THE CHURCH AND THE CHRISTIAN

OTHER BOOKS BY SHAILER MATHEWS

HISTORICAL

Select Mediaeval Documents
The French Revolution, 1789–1815
New Testament Times in Palestine
The Spiritual Interpretation of History
The Validity of American Ideals
The Making of Tomorrow
The Messianic Hope in the New Testament

SOCIAL ASPECTS OF CHRISTIANITY

Jesus on Social Institutions
The Social Gospel
The Individual and the Social Gospel
The Church and the Changing Order
Christianity and Social Process
Creative Christianity
Patriotism and Religion

RELIGIOUS BELIEF

The Growth of the Idea of God
The Atonement and the Social Process
Immortality and the Cosmic Process
The Gospel and the Modern Man
The Faith of Modernism
Contributions of Science to Religion
  With Thirteen Scientists
A Dictionary of Religion and Ethics
  With G. B. Smith
A Constructive Life of Christ
  With E. D. Burton
The Student's Gospels
  With E. J. Goodspeed

New Faith For Old: An Autobiography

THE CHURCH

AND THE

CHRISTIAN

By

SHAILER MATHEWS

NEW YORK
THE MACMILLAN COMPANY
1938

PRINTED IN THE UNITED STATES OF AMERICA
AMERICAN BOOK—STRATFORD PRESS, INC., NEW YORK

Contents

CHAPTER   PAGE

1. *The Ecclesiastical Conception of "the Church"*   1

2. *Churches as Religious Social Groups*   12

3. *Churches and "the Church"*   27

4. *The Christ of the Churches*   54

5. *A Church as a Channel of Grace*   75

6. *Churches as Moral Ferments*   103

7. *Are Churches Still Needed?*   139

THE CHURCH AND THE CHRISTIAN

I

THE ECCLESIASTICAL CONCEPTION OF "THE CHURCH"

FOR HALF A CENTURY AND more, Christians have been taking an inventory of their religious assets. The first to come within the range of such accounting was the Bible itself, then the historical Jesus, then his teaching and its applicability to modern society, then the psychology and history of religion. Now the Church is the center of attention.

Such an inventory was inevitable among Protestants. In making the Bible the sole authoritative revelation of truth they were especially vulnerable to historical literary criticism. In the effort to go behind Confessional orthodoxy, they first went "back to Jesus," but in attempting to apply his teaching to the modern world, they confronted economic and political situations radically different from those of the time in which he taught. The New Testament was discovered to be a literature resulting from the application of faith in Jesus to a contemporary civilization. Like the Old Testament, its authority decreased as a collection of infallible oracles. "The Church," as a concrete element of the Christian religion, became a final court of last appeal.

For Christian bodies claiming catholicity this was, of course, nothing new. They had always recognized "the Church" as having authority, not only to interpret the Bible, but to supplement its revelation by the authority resident in the "Bride of Christ." But to Protestant communities which had sprung up during and after the Reformation, the recognition of "the Church" as a concrete agent of Christianity has almost the novelty of discovery and even of a heresy. Especially in America, where the rise of denominations and sects had been the natural accompaniment of democracy, the new Church-consciousness aroused both enthusiasm and uncertainty. On the one side was the vehement restatement of the Protestant orthodoxies, with a refusal to recognize the right of religious bodies to modernize their theological formulas; and, on the other, the insistence that "the Church," as a synonym of organized Christianity, had duties to social institutions and cultural processes which necessitated the reinterpretation of formulas. To one group of Protestants, doctrines were superior to "the Church." To others, "the Church" was an institution having obligations which had little dependence upon theology. The term indeed became practically synonymous with Christianity itself. "All who accept Jesus Christ as son of God and their Lord and Savior, and realize their dependence upon God's mercy revealed in him have in that fact a supernatural bond of oneness which subsists in spite of divergencies in defining the divine mystery of the Lord." So declared the Edinburgh Conference on Faith and Order.

It was once rather fashionable among the more liberal Protestant theologians to distinguish sharply between Christianity and what they call "Churchianity." To them Christianity lost very largely institutional significance; it had an essence which had suffered the buffetings of ecclesiastics from Paul to Calvin. It became a search for truth supplemented by a more or less rationalized mysticism. For the less theologically minded, a church had a vestigially religious value, and was identified with untenable doctrines professed by a group of people who met with some regularity for the purpose of hearing the choir sing to them and the minister pray for them and preach to them. The continuity of such a church depended to a large degree upon a Sunday School which adolescent youth abandoned, Boy Scouts, women's societies, and if a church was large, literary classes and basket-ball teams. Such activities were justified on the ground that they served to maintain the interest of the persons concerned in a church, and at the same time served the welfare of the community. If the waters of the swimming pool were stirred more frequently than the waters of the baptistry, a church could still live in the hope that the morale of its community was maintained at a higher plane than would have been otherwise possible.

3

Incidentally, "the Church" became a Jack-of-all-reforms.

I should be the last to belittle the importance of social activities on the part of a church, but I am convinced that unless it is more than a community center for recreation and social acquaintance, a church is not fulfilling its historic function. With the exception of Judaism, Christianity is unique in that it has such an institution. Buddhism has its priesthood, Hinduism its castes, Mohammedanism its mosques, but no one of them has an institution like the Christian Church. Protestantism needs a new appreciation of what a church as an institution means to the Christian religion. Especially does the modernist need to guard against letting his interest in the restatement of Christian values cause him to overlook its significance. It may very well be that the conditions of membership in such an organization need to be revised, but those who desire to make the Christian faith more intelligible should not neglect that central religious character which a church has always claimed.

I

The Second World Conference on Faith and Order, held in Edinburgh, in 1937, declared that "The Church is the body of Christ and the blessed company of faithful people, whether in heaven or on earth, the communion of saints. It is the function of the Church to glorify God in its life and worship, to proclaim the Gospel to every creature, to build up in the fellowship and the life of the Spirit all believing people of every race and nation. To this end God bestows his grace in the Church on its members through his Word and Sacraments, and in the abiding presence of the Holy Spirit." The report goes on, however, to say that "Different churches differ in their use of the term 'church.' Some would apply the term not only to the visible, redeemed, and redemptive community, but also to the invisible company of the fully redeemed; For only when the word is used in this sense would it be right to say, 'extra ecclesiam nulla salus.' Others regard the term 'church' with reference to this invisible company of true Christians known only to God as misleading and unscriptural."

Little attention was paid by this Conference to the democratic conception of the term as referring to local bodies as distinct from the Catholic conception of a unity of believers which has suffered schism.

Other definitions of the term abound. It may denote all those who "from the beginning of the world have believed in the one true God and have been made his children by grace." Such a definition includes dead as well as living Christians. The commonly accepted definition of the term by Catholics is that of Bellarmine: "A body of men united together by the profession of the same Christian faith, and by participation in the same Christian sacraments, under

5

the governance of lawful pastors, more especially of the Roman pontiff, the sole vicar of Christ on earth." The condition of membership in such a body is, first, profession of the true faith, which is a revelation of the son of God explicitly or implicitly made by all that the Church teaches; second, baptism; third, submission to the authority of the Church and its appointed rulers; fourth, the participation in the right to communion with the Church. The Church interprets these views generously in the case of heretics who have been baptized and have not voluntarily renounced the Catholic faith. They are members of the Church internally. The secret heresy does not necessarily separate the Christian from the Church. The same is true of schism. The Church recognizes the schismatic as a member entitled to her communion until by open and notorious rebellion he rejects her authority. It follows naturally that the Church, if thus conceived, can never become corrupt in faith or in morals, or lose the priesthood or the sacraments. This so-called gift of "indefectibility" does not protect the Church from defection of heretics, but such heretics when organized in churches do not carry the prerogatives shared by the see of Rome.

Protestant theologians have defined the term in such a way as to break the conception of Catholic unity except in an invisible Church. Calvin says that the Church is to be found "where the word of God is preached in its purity, and the sacraments administered according to Christ's ordinance." The Westminster Confession affirms that the Church "consists of all those throughout the world that profess the true religion, together with their children." Dr. A. H. Strong, a Baptist, defined the Church as "the whole company of regenerate persons in all times and ages, in heaven and on earth." In this sense the Church is identical with the spiritual kingdom of God, and is invisible.

In a more concrete sense the term may indicate "the smaller company of regenerate persons who in any given community unite themselves voluntarily together in accordance with Christ's laws for the purpose of securing the complete establishment of his Kingdom in themselves and in the world." This definition Dr. Strong expands as follows: "The laws of Christ to which people unite themselves into churches are, first, the Scriptures as the sole rule of doctrine and polity, credible evidence of regeneration, immersion, the dependence in the participation in the Lord's Supper upon former baptism by immersion, the democratic form of government, responsibility of a church solely to Christ, freedom of the individual conscience, total independence of the church and state." According to Dr. Strong, bodies of Christians who refuse to accept these principles may be called churches, but cannot be regarded as in all respects organized according to Christ's law. "It is only courtesy," he says, "to speak of pedobaptist organizations as churches."

II

Such definitions are the self-estimate of Christian organizations. Whether they come from Rome or from Baptists, they express a theological chauvinism which has made co-operation between Christian bodies difficult, if not impossible. They serve to justify a claim to the monopoly of divinely revealed truth, the right to exclude those holding "false doctrine," the authority to set the conditions of God's salvation of sinners. They presuppose fear of divine punishment on the part of individuals and social organizations.

Whether or not one agrees with such ecclesiastical formulas, any student of Western civilization knows the influence of organized religious bodies claiming to represent the will of the deity and declaring the conditions upon which eternal bliss or misery depends. Fear may not have "made the gods," but it has helped to make orthodoxy. Churches and sects alike have been pressure-groups. For the difference which has been drawn between churches and sects is here negligible. Whether a group represents a continuous institutional life or seeks to cut loose from history and re-establish the Christian community of the New Testament, it regards itself as expressing the divine will, and possessing an authoritative revelation.

But these definitions do something more. They serve to distinguish between Christianity as a religious system and groups of Christians. This distinction is not always made. The duties which belong to Christians, as individuals, are easily transferred to "the Church." It needs no exceptional powers of observation to discover the confusion to which such neglect of definition leads. If "the Church" is to be treated as a synonym of the Christian religion, clear thinking is difficult; but when it is called upon to face duties which are as concrete as industry and social reform, confusion becomes worse confounded. The obligations of individuals are transferred to "the Church." No distinction is drawn between the obligations of individual Christians and of churches as social groups having a definite function. What seems to be particularly needed at the present time is an understanding of Christian groups. We can speak of an ecumenical Christianity, but a Holy Catholic Church which has no organization, and includes the dead as well as the living, is clearly a figure of speech. What it represents must be found in history.

III

These definitions also recognize the fact that Christians are real persons with social tendencies. Christianity is not something that exists, like the forces of the universe, distinct from Christians. To understand its doctrines it is necessary to know the conditions in which the makers of the doctrines lived, their behavior in everyday life, and the cultural tensions which they had to resolve. Strictly speaking, there is no history of Christianity. There is only the history of Christians. The organization and function of a church are not revealed from heaven but are aspects of that social behavior which the word Christianity connotes. Individuals are affected by membership in churches, but the churches, both in practice and in doctrine, quite as truly perpetuate the religious habits, preconceptions, hopes and fears of individual Christians. Only as one ceases to think of abstractions can one understand that every religion is a more or less organized form of behavior in which human beings undertake to get help from that supernatural Power upon which they feel themselves dependent. The conceptions of that Power, the techniques by which its assistance is gained, are derived from the cultural, economic, and other elements of a social order. Of no religion is this truer than of the religion of those who call themselves Christians because they seek supernatural assistance through the acceptance of Jesus Christ as revealer of divine love. Churches are social agents of that quest. Their history is as concrete as that of states. Christianity as a religion has developed within them. Its origin, its institutions, its thought patterns, have been conditioned by their participation as social groups in the economic, political, social processes of the Western world. That Western civilization should have given rise to churches is due to its own character. "The Church" may be used as a labor-saving but sociologically inaccurate term to represent Christianity in general, but churches must be studied from the point of view of our growing knowledge that a social order is a group of groups having different functions which condition one another and the individuals who compose them.

2

CHURCHES AS RELIGIOUS SOCIAL GROUPS

CHURCHES ARE GROUPS OF Christians formed to organize their lives with help from God through a relationship determined by faith in Jesus Christ. That religious purpose is their determined function. They are means of adjusting their members and such others as they may influence with cosmic activity.

The study of Christianity, like that of any religion, is a study of social psychology dealing with the function, the beliefs, the organization, the practices, and the influence of religious groups. The first step in such a study is to consider how churches have been formed.

I

A group is formed to accomplish collectively what its members could not accomplish otherwise. It has a continuous subconscious life, preserving, and to some extent, determining, the attitudes, beliefs, and practices of its members. A group is continuous, sur-

viving successive changes in its constituency. Men
join it as an on-going entity. Formulas, whether political, scientific, educational, or religious, are rooted
in this unconscious level. Every association tends to
express its function in an orthodoxy, the acceptance
of which becomes a test of membership. In so far as
individuals participate in the activities of a group,
they acknowledge its function. In the course of time,
variant opinions of its members may rationalize a
group's basic attitudes more effectively and replace
or supplement older formulas and practices, but
such changes must not contradict the basic group-
function. Otherwise they destroy the unity and the
permanence of the group itself.

The function of religious groups is conditioned by
belief. Where a religion centers about a founder, this
faith involves loyalty to the interpretation placed
upon him by the group. An attempt to account
rationally for such a revelatory person serves to deprive the group of its sense of function. Any recast-
ing of the formulas and practices in which this loyalty has been expressed threatens the abandonment
of values embodied in previous group action. That is
why attempts to modify the Christology of the
churches meet with vigorous opposition. If the Nicene formula be abandoned in the interest of some
new interpretation of Jesus, the whole structure of
orthodoxy built up by continuous Christian groups
seems threatened.

To understand the history of Christianity it is,

therefore, of first importance to discover historically the function and the structure of groups of Christians. The history of churches and sects is more than a record of beliefs set forth by various Christians. These may deserve attention in themselves, but they represent Christianity as a religion only as they are appropriated and expressed by bodies of Christians. Until this is done, they are only individual interpretations of group beliefs.

II

A social order is composed of groups, each organized for the accomplishment of certain ends. These groups are related to one another, and changes within one are likely to affect the character of others. Social process is largely determined by this inter-action.

In such a process there develops what may be roughly called a social mind and a counter-social mind. The former is the resultant of the combination of dominant group interests and pressures. The counter-social mind is the expression of ideas and tendencies which do not become dominant but may ultimately affect social process. The dominant social mind tends towards uniformity, groups with different functions tending to reproduce the same ideas, attitudes, and practices. In an imperialistic world coerced unity will be a presupposition in group life. Nationalistic, democratic, socialistic social orders will find their respective presuppositions appearing in all group life which is permitted to exist.

Thus the permanence of a group is dependent not only upon its success in inter-group adjustment, but upon its relation to social trends.

Speaking generally, the relation of groups passes through the stages of isolation, unadjusted contact, interaction which is frequently one of opposition and even conflict, consequent adjustment determined by a variety of forces, some of them unpredictable. Unless it results in the destruction of one or both of the groups concerned, opposition develops a group's solidarity and permanence. But a group cannot exist in such absolute isolation as neither to affect nor be affected by the other groups with which it is in contact. Its permanence will depend upon how necessary its function is. When the needs for which a group has come into being are satisfied or outgrown, the group will either go out of existence or have a vestigial or sentimental value. When groups subject to similar forces of change—geographic, climatic, economic or political—come into contact with one another, the adjustment will be mutual. Such adjustment will sometimes be given the unfriendly name of compromise, but more often it is an element of a social process itself, and serves to preserve at least some of the values represented by the contacting groups.

Especially is its permanence of function tested when a group becomes a nucleus of an alien religion

in another civilization. The history of Mohammedanism in non-Arabian civilizations, of Buddhism in
China and Japan, of Judaism in various nations,
illustrates how a religious group adjusts itself to new
conditions without abandoning its dominant and, as
believed, supernaturally given function. The fate of
an alien religion in a new environment is dependent
upon the degree to which it is adjustable with the
group life of the civilization into which it has come.
In the case of Christianity, groups carrying forward
an aspect of Jewish religion expressed in the Messianic valuation of Jesus, came into a non-Jewish
world. Historic Christianity began in the adjustment
of groups accepting this alien religion to the groups
representing the politics, social trends, and religions
of the Greco-Roman world. It thus became a factor
in the social process from which Western civilization
emerged.

III

The belief that a church was founded by Jesus is
correct in that he founded a group of Jews who followed him in the expectation that he would fulfill
their hopes of a glorious and divinely established
Jewish empire. Jesus could speak of his followers as
constituting an *ecclesia*, or community, and it was as
a leader of such a following that he was executed.
This community seems to have had a rudimentary
organization, but nothing resembling the institution

which developed from it or indeed any quality that could threaten loyalty to the Mosaic religion. We have no evidence that Jesus planned to establish an independent religion. He shared in the worship of the synagogue and the Temple; he declared that he had not come to destroy the Law and the prophets; he said that he had been sent to the lost sheep of the house of Israel. It did not occur to his immediate disciples to abandon their ancestral religion. In so far as we can recover the history of the early days, the community which he founded was a Jewish sect whose chief characteristic was its members' belief that their crucified Master was the Christ, who had risen from the dead and ascended into a not distant heaven, from which he was presently to return to judge the world and set up the kingdom of God.

For after the death of Jesus, his followers' faith became more than a reminiscence. It was a ground of hope for acquittal at a coming Judgment and a condition of sharing what they regarded as super-natural power. The Holy Spirit which had enabled Jesus to combat the forces of evil, cast out demons, cure diseases, and rise from the dead came upon the members of the community which he had founded. The account of this experience given in the book of Acts shows that it was not dependent upon action of the church or always that of the apostles, but upon the acceptance of Jesus as Messiah. While it usually followed the profession of this faith by bap-tism, it was not derived from the rite. Each indi-

vidual Christian had personal access to God, and as-
surance of acquittal at the approaching Judgment.

A community was formed by those who shared
this hope and had this experience of God. Believing
as they did that the world was under the control of
Satan and was coming to an end during their own
lifetime, Christian Jews identified their acquittal at
the coming Judgment with a triumph over mortality.
The community apparently made no ritual treatment of the crucifixion as a sacrifice. The resurrection was the basis of hope. Like Jesus, his followers
would be raised from the abode of departed spirits,
or changed without dying, into a mode of spiritual
life which he already enjoyed. When he appeared
they would be like him.

This hope became the content of the Gospel, a
promise of an acquittal at the coming Judgment, of
a deliverance from death and of eternal joy for
those who believed it. Association of those who held
it formed the primitive Christian church in Jerusalem.

IV

The beginning of Christianity as an independent
religion is to be seen in the emergence in Syria and
Asia Minor of groups who accepted this message
of Jewish enthusiasts. A growing number of men
and women within the Roman Empire were dis-
satisfied with conventional polytheism. Such per-

sons were particularly susceptible to the influence of Oriental and Semitic religions. From these "God-fearers" who had accepted the monotheism of Judaism the membership of the new groups were largely drawn. By the end of the first century their Jewish members had disappeared, Judaism had become ethnic, the Christian groups had become Gentile, Jewish hope for the "Kingdom of God" was sublimated into an eschatology which all might share without regard to sex or birth. In the scattered groups of believers a new religion had been born.

So far as we can judge from the literary remains of the first century, because of its belittling of the social order in which they lived, Christians were in danger of duplicating the excesses of many religious groups who claimed to experience the divine power. Because of the "gift of the Holy Spirit," they could speak with tongues and work miracles. They were tempted to become celibate, abandon the economic world and live on charity. Some Christians did so live, but those who formed the basis of the Christian movement were saved from fanaticism by the sanity of the apostle Paul. He shared in their reliance upon supernatural power, which he claimed to possess himself, but he saw the moral implications of the impact of the divine upon the human. The new life which Christians were to enjoy in the coming kingdom was one of love, and this new life had already begun in their experience. Their personality had been so changed by contact with the divine as not only to be superior to death, but to be under the moral inspiration of the divine Spirit. Christians were to live in the present age as they might expect to live in the age to come.

As a form of social behavior intended to gain help from superhuman power, the new movement was a genuine religion and not a philosophy. In fact, these early Christians were warned against philosophy and urged to center their attention upon following the impulses of the Spirit. Their common faith and religious experience led them to meet together and share their hopes and enthusiasms. Such organization as they had was simple, modeled upon that of the synagogue with which the original Christians of Palestine had been familiar. But this organization was itself, according to Paul, under supernatural direction. The Spirit of Jesus had given the members of the group a variety of tasks and corresponding efficiencies. While some might be of more honor than others, all offices were the gift of the same Spirit. To use Paul's striking figure, Christians were to regard themselves as members of the body of Christ, each as necessary for its perfection as the eye is to the physical body. Thus from the very inception of Christianity, a church had a distinctly religious function. It was a community of those who were experiencing the power of God, and enjoying the reconciliation with him which their acceptance of Jesus as Lord made possible. Any objective study of Christianity must recognize that its history is the history of these religious groups. But their reliance upon supernatural revelation, and their belief that they had been founded by an incarnate God, did not free them from sociology. The development of Christianity as an independent religion was due to the interaction of groups of Christians with the other groups and the social trends of successive social orders.

V

The first contact of the Christian groups with those of the Roman Empire illustrated a common reaction: they attempted isolation. The later New Testament writers abound in the contrast between the believer and "the world," that is to say, the total social order in the midst of which the Christians lived. This world was under the control of Satan, and was evil. The Christians were to keep themselves unspotted from it. As those who were to judge angels, they were not even to appeal to courts. Under the influence of religious practices drawn from the Far East, various types of asceticism developed, and monks and nuns detached themselves from the other elements of the developing Christian movement, to find security from the evil world in the desert or the mountains.

Such a defeatist spirit was consistent with the Christian concern with other-worldly salvation, but most groups of Christians within the different cities of the Empire instead of withdrawing from the world, continued in the world. The general laws of group adjustment were evident. Conditioning the process was the fact that the churches were composed of people who although they believed themselves citizens of a coming kingdom, unlike monks and hermits, maintained their occupations and social contacts. It was natural, therefore, for Christian groups to hold firmly to their own solidarity as determined by their origin and function. Scattered in the cities of the Roman Empire, they developed their own habits and style of dress, customs, institutional rites and organization. They cared for their poor, widows, orphans, and those who were imprisoned on account of their faith; though not seeking to end slavery, their members treated slaves as brothers; they exchanged letters with their fellow churches; they disciplined those who had broken their customs or denied their teaching; they developed a cult which was more than religious pageantry. Their members exorcised demons in the name of Christ, they were said even to raise the dead. They regarded themselves as a third race co-ordinate with Jews and pagans.

VI

Group solidarity was furthered by the pressure of the state. The refusal of Christians to share in the political religion of Rome made them political suspects. Christianity, unlike Judaism, was not an officially recognized religion of the Empire, and political suspicion was reinforced by the hostility of other religious groups with which the empire abounded. Until the time of Decius at the end of the third century, and Diocletian in the beginning of the fourth there was no general persecution, but the governors of different provinces or the magistrates of different cities might arrest and punish, often by death, those who admitted they were Christians. When there was an empire-wide attempt to crush the Christian movement, loyalty to the religion was dangerous. Many Christians, in terror of their lives, became apostates. Yet the Christian groups were so permanently established as to be real factors in political programs and only a few years after the attempt of Diocletian to extirpate Christianity, Constantine gave it legal standing and himself, on his deathbed, was baptized. The question as to whether apostates should be received back into the Church became a source of factional dispute which by the end of the fourth century had led to a conception of churches as composed of those who, professing faith in Christ, were not necessarily possessed of a thoroughly Christian morality.

More important, however, than this external pressure in building up the solidarity of the Christian groups was their basic faith in Jesus as the Savior. The confession of this faith did not, however, express all the beliefs which Christians held. Origen, in his *De Principiis*, gives a summary of what the

Christians commonly believed. These include a belief: (1) in one God who created and arranged all things, but no certainty as to whether he can be said to be incorporeal; (2) in Jesus Christ, born of the Father before all creatures, who became a man incarnate but remained God, who was born of the Virgin and of the Holy Spirit, died, rose, and ascended into heaven; (3) in the Holy Spirit associated in honor and dignity with the Father and the Son; (4) in a soul having a substance and life of its own, to be punished or rewarded after death, when it will have been united to the body which has been raised; (5) in the existence of the devil and his angels, but without any distinct statement as to their nature; (6) in the destruction of the world on account of its wickedness, but without any clear statement as to what will exist after the earth's destruction; (7) in the inspiration of the Scriptures which have both obvious and a spiritually esoteric meaning; (8) in the existence of angels, but with no opinion as to whether the sun, moon, and stars are living beings.

Such a statement shows that Christian doctrine was Biblically centered and that the churches did not hold essential the scientific and pseudo-scientific ideas of the times. A creedal statement probably used as a confession of faith at baptism was the real basis of group solidarity. In its earliest form it was known as the old Roman Symbol or Rule of Faith which became the nucleus of ecumenical Christian doctrine. This Roman Confession probably ran as follows:

I believe in God the Father almighty, and in Jesus Christ his own begotten son, our Lord, born of the Holy Ghost and Mary the Virgin, crucified under Pontius Pilate and buried; and the third day he rose from the dead, ascended into heaven, sits on the right hand of the Father, whence he will come to judge the living and the dead; and in the Holy Ghost, the Holy Church, the forgiveness of sins, the resurrection of the flesh.

This consciousness of a common belief contributed to the maintenance of group solidarity as churches interacted with other elements of social orders which produced Western civilization. At the end of the first century the churches were composed of adults who had lived in the atmosphere of polytheism. In becoming Christians they could not altogether break with their religious experience and those political institutions that formed the background of their life. In joining a Christian group they committed themselves to its basic belief in Jesus, but in organizing the group to fulfill its function, their social inheritance furnished patterns of thought and techniques for religious practices.

Christians did not intentionally build up a religious syncretism. The difference between the Christianity of the Jewish community and that of the churches of the third century was due to social process. The law of group adjustment is obvious. Only thus can we understand how the Christian movement, while supplanting the worship of the major gods, preserved the minor divinities of Roman and Teutonic paganism in its saints. Converts to Christianity could not give up their fear of and reliance upon local deities, or the festivals of Judaism and paganism. In the course of time such practices became identified with Christianity and had to be rationalized and brought into line with the function of churches to mediate Jesus as a revealer of salvation to mankind. Many of these practices would not have been derived from a modern world, but they became elements of the Christian religion which the modern world has inherited. Christianity as a religion was the work of followers of Jesus Christ who formed groups which preserved their solidarity by doctrinal tests. Thus, dogma was born. But a shared religious experience was older than dogma.

3

CHURCHES AND
"THE CHURCH"

THE EARLY CHRISTIAN
groups possessed no unity of organization. Not only
did different regions of the Roman Empire have
their own bishops and councils, but they had also
groups differing as to the nature of the Christianity
they professed. Indeed, so evident was this lack of
unity that Celsus, a most effective enemy of Christianity, declared that Christians were "divided and
split up into factions, each individual desiring to
have his own party." Origen admits the existence of
different sects, but accounts for them by the desire
of scholars to enter more profoundly into the truths
of Christianity. A mere catalogue of heresies shows
the lack of Christian unity in the early days of
Christianity. Christian minorities were condemned
as heretics. "The Church" was the victorious group
that gave no recognition to dissent.

Two tendencies are to be seen in groups having
the same function. However independent they may
have been originally, in the course of time they tend
to give rise to a generic concept for which a term be-

comes a watchword. The state, democracy, the labor movement, and countless other terms illustrate this tendency. It was natural, therefore, for the word "Church," which originally indicated a local community of Christians, to acquire a generic content as different Christian groups spread across the Roman Empire.

A second characteristic of the generalizing of a generic term is the tendency towards personification. This is familiar enough in the popular use of personal names like Uncle Sam or John Bull to represent nations. In the case of the Christian churches, this process of personification is to be seen in the New Testament. The Church is spoken of as the bride of Christ; it is a body of which the individual Christians are members; it is the family of God. Such personification often results in the characteristics of an individual being attributed to the group and an original conception is supplemented and expanded by inappropriate ideas, practices and institutions. In spite of such anthropomorphism the basic function of the Christian communities was retained. The church, whether local or generic, was a group of those who through their faith in Jesus were drawing upon the divine power. It not only carried in itself faith in Jesus as the Savior but also it became a channel of divine power. Such a conception of a church was not derived from philosophical deduction but from the attitudes and practices of Christians. Churches became authoritative in that they

were popularly felt to express and preserve the experience of God which followed the acceptance of
Jesus as officially interpreted.

II

A new collectivism was furthered by the conscious
solidarity of Christian groups. Contemporary practices entered into their organization but its basic pattern was that of the Jewish synagogue, an institution
of prayer and instruction, without sacrifices, the officials of which were not priests but laymen. The
Christian churches became centers of instruction, or
illumination, as Justin Martyr calls it, and prayer.
In so far as any reference is made to sacrifice, it is
that of Jesus on the Cross. Their officials were
known as presbyters or elders, and not priests. In
fact, it is not until the middle of the third century
that the word, priest, is used by Cyprian in the case
of the bishop. As the churches grew the need of organization became greater, and there emerged from
the group of presbyters one who was known as the
bishop. Those who, like Ignatius, wished to prevent
the Christian communities from disintegrating into
competitive groups, found the center of solidarity
in doctrine with the bishop as its preserver. The
churches were to remain loyal to the bishops, who,
in turn, were loyal to the apostolic tradition.

The administrative organization of the Empire
made it natural for the bishops of the municipal

churches of different provinces or districts to meet in some metropolis, which thus became a center of joint action on the part of the groups. These councils became the regulators of the life of the churches and determined what should be regarded as proper exposition of the apostolic inheritance. Continuity in group attitude was thus assured. Bishops and churches holding to doctrinal positions judged by these councils as inconsistent with the inherited belief preserved by the various churches were disciplined by whatever means were available to a religion that was not licensed by imperial authority.

Such reliance upon the apostolic heritage demanded a literature coming from apostolic circles. The Old Testament as the embodiment of divine revelation was by general consent regarded as authoritative, by Christians as well as Jews; but there was a growing Christian literature which purported to represent the teaching of Jesus and the apostles. Much of this was distinctly propagandist, intended to justify some heretical teaching. Some of it was composed of reminiscences of Jesus as organized by churches in different parts of the Empire. By the middle of the second century, the need of settling doctrinal disputes by appeal to an authoritative literature unquestionably from the apostles led to the selection of certain books which became the measuring rod, or the canon, of doctrine. Successive councils in different parts of the Empire made different selections, but by a sort of general consent the Four

Gospels, the thirteen Epistles of Paul, the book of
Acts, I Peter and I John were accepted as apostolic
and authoritative. Different groups of churches
added various other authoritative writings, and there
sprang up various canons in different parts of the
Empire. In 397 A.D. the third Council of Carthage
selected the writings now to be found in the New
Testament of the Roman and Protestant churches.
The West accepted the list, but no General Council
ratified it until Trent in the sixteenth century. In the
East, there were several canons, some longer and
some shorter than the Western. Incidentally, it may
be added that similar differences have appeared as
to the canon of authoritative literature that came
over from Judaism. Acceptance of the Hebrew Old
Testament or the Greek version, the Septuagint,
which contained the Apocrypha, determined the
choice.

But, as it will be shown in a later chapter, the chief
matter of debate was as to how the functional faith
in Jesus as the divine Savior was to be rationalized.
Most of the differences here arose from the contemporary philosophical and religious practices and beliefs. Some authority was felt to be needed by the
churches lest their common character should be lost.
Elements upon which authority could be based were
present by the end of the third century, in the Scriptures, the bishops and the councils. But beneath all
such organized authority was the subconscious life
of Christian communities composed of those who

31

had already vocabularies and practices guaranteeing group solidarity and continuity. This basic group life, rather than philosophical discussion, was the final court of appeal. Not philosophy, but the religious behavior and attitude of Christians expressed in the continuous groups, was to prove the determining factor in shaping Christianity. True Christian doctrine was that which had always, everywhere, and by all been believed. That such a test was historically indefensible did not concern those who had been victorious in the century-long struggle with dissenting groups of Christians. That such struggle too often exhibited the immoral and even sadistic traits of Christians was obscured by ecclesiastical definitions and assumptions of divine guidance. Christians organized their councils and anathematized their defeated brethren with as little regard for the ethics of him whom they declared to be of the same substance as God the Father, as if the Sermon on the Mount had never been delivered.

III

It was natural that early Christian groups in a geographical area having the same formulas should have gravitated towards each other. In so doing they followed existing economic and political trends in population. Churches within an administrative district gathered around its metropolitan center, and in course of time this unification reflected the relations of the imperial system to the entire Empire. Catholicity was the religious equivalent of imperialism. As such, it shared different currents in the Roman state.

In the Eastern half imperialism was superimposed upon nations and civilizations which were old when Rome was founded. The emperors were wise enough not to attempt more. The provinces respected national histories, and the metropolitan centers were not deprived of such economic and cultural importance as they had already attained. Imperialism in the Near East, therefore, conserved, rather than created, social orders. The attempt of Constantine and his successors to transfer the center of imperial unity from Rome to Constantinople served to separate the East from the West. This separation is to be seen in the history of the Eastern churches. Each metropolis became the center of an ecclesiastical unit which never yielded much more than a gesture of polite respect to the bishops either of Constantinople or of Rome. They became Patriarchates. Their constituent bishops might meet in councils which claimed to be ecumenical, but the Patriarchates held to ecclesiastical imperialism no more than had the various nations of the East been detached from their ethnic and political inheritances. The Eastern churches became the preservers of the ecclesiastical *status quo,* which was reached by the time of the Moslem invasion. There were no creative social or political movements in the East with which Christian communities could interact. As groups within a hostile environ-

ment the Christian churches of the East have preserved not only a common faith, but also their ancient
ethnic and metropolitan independence. The extension
of Eastern Christianity into the Balkans and Russia
added new ecclesiastical units. These various Patriarchates have maintained themselves not only as opposed to Moslem masters, but as independent of the
Roman Catholic Church and of one another.

In the West, however, Roman imperialism, from
the time of Julius Caesar, was creative. A new civilization was shaped up in conquered territory. In such
a process, Rome was more than a name. It was not
only the one great city of the West, but it was the
center of administrative and cultural influence. The
bishoprics of the West to a considerable extent followed the various administrative lines of the empire
and did not regard themselves as equal with Rome.
Even the inundation of the West by the Teutonic
tribes, did not altogether destroy these inheritances
of an imperial system. Local councils were composed
of the bishops in various areas, but the bishop of
Rome steadily became a center of ecclesiastical unity.
North Africa under the influence of Cyprian recognized his superiority. His influence was increased by
the catastrophes of the early Middle Ages, and al-
leged historical basis was given to his temporal
power by the so-called *Donation of Constantine,* now
generally recognized as a forgery, and the *Decretals*
of Isidore, the genuineness of which is no longer
held. Imperialism was embodied in the social de-

34

velopment of the West and Roman Catholicism
might be described as a transcendentalized empire,
preserving much of the administrative machinery
and the legal points of view of its imperial pattern.

In its earliest stages the imperial concept of Catholic Christianity was not affected by geographical
considerations. Constantine had discovered the political possibilities within Christianity and, without
professed conversion, took over responsibility for
the affairs of the churches. This was natural in view
of his constitutional standing as Pontifex Maximus
No phase of the life of the Empire could expect to
escape imperial control. To Constantine and his successors, religion was one aspect of the State. They
saw in ecclesiastical controversies danger to the imperial unity. Not only was the great mass of citizens
pagan, but within the churches themselves, there
were constant dissensions. If these had been merely
theological, like the quarrels between the schools of
philosophy, they probably would not have attracted
the attention of the emperors; but doctrines became
rallying cries for parties. Repeatedly, they led to
popular disturbances, and threatened the peace of
cities and districts. This was particularly the case in
the Arian controversy. The churches of the eastern
half of the Empire were engaged in a bitter controversy which gave rise to tumults that neither bishops
nor governors seemed able to quiet. The emperor
urged the disputants to agree, but failing, decided to
get a formula which could be enforced among all the

churches of the Empire. He therefore called the first general council of the Christian churches at Nicea in 325. There, although he had never been baptized, he presided as "the bishop of bishops." In a series of meetings sometimes marked by physical violence, a formula was adopted which expanded the old Roman Symbol by terms which declared that the Son was the same substance as the Father, very God of very God, begotten, not created. This formula, through the influence of the State, was to be adopted by all Christian churches. Catholicism was orthodoxy enforced by the Empire. It was never coextension with the beliefs of all Christian groups.

The history of the Nicene formula illustrates how true it is that orthodoxy is an authoritative formula enforced by a dominant party. At one time, Arianism was supported by the State. Rival councils simultaneously anathematized and adopted the decision of Nicea. For centuries, the emperors undertook to control the actions of the various Patriarchates and so far succeeded as to develop within the eastern half of the Empire new elements of orthodoxy involving the nature, person, and will of Christ. In these controversies, the influence of the bishops of Rome was sometimes felt, but the politics of the Empire, which increasingly involved the control of the churches, often brought the emperors and popes into direct opposition. The western churches were little affected by the theological speculations of the eastern bishops. They were loyal to the Nicene formula and their theology became a Catholicism furthered by the Teutonic states in western Europe. Arianism had been adopted by the Goths who swept over into Gaul and northern Africa, not because they were theologically minded, but because they had been converted by Arian Christians. There was a strong probability that the churches of Gaul and northern Italy would become Arian. The political effect of such a theological outcome is not difficult to imagine. But thanks to the sagacity and personality of the popes, the Franks became adherents to the Church of Rome and promptly proceeded to subdue Arian tribes like the Lombards. After Charlemagne, imperialism assured the permanence in western Europe not only of Nicene orthodoxy, but of Roman Catholicism.

IV

This fact is of supreme importance in the development of Christianity.

When the classical civilization disintegrated under the armed immigration of Teutonic tribes, the Roman Church was about the only organization that survived. During the centuries of continuous struggle and tribal warfare it preserved the concept of unity which imperialism had developed. But it was none the less subject to influences of other social groups. Feudalism involved church officials in social institutions and practices. Bishops and abbots held great sections of territory under the feudal system.

It was inevitable that the question should arise as to who invested them with their authority. Did it come from their spiritual or from their feudal lord? In the struggle which followed, the logic of the two contending parties was equally sound, and the Concordat which resulted, to the effect that the king or emperor should invest the ecclesiastical feudal lord with his temporal power, and the pope should invest him with the spiritual appointment, seems to have been the only way out of an otherwise endless controversy. In this process the distinction between spiritual and temporal interests was sharply drawn and served to clarify, at least in theory, the function of the Church as a religious organization. But imperialism survived its appropriation of feudal elements. The Church of the West increasingly consolidated its administration and gained power as one of the elements of a social order which gradually passed from reliance upon military service and land tenure to nationalism and unconstitutional monarchy.

The contact of the Church with the feudal social order followed the general law of group contact which had obtained under very different conditions in the Roman Empire. Feudal conceptions were taken over into the growing theological structure, and the pattern in which the relations of man and the deity were pictured was drawn from the combination of imperialism and feudalism which marked European society. All served to give new significance to the Roman Church and to develop it as an organization which, in theory at least, not only furnished the truth of revelation, but served as the effective representative of deity. Catholicity in the western world was centered in the papacy, and therefore was separated from the Catholicity represented by the eastern churches. By means of its immediate relation with the political authorities, the Church suppressed dissent from its authority, and heretics were exterminated as far as it was possible. Religious enthusiasm gave sanction to vast military crusades, holy wars were preached, and kings were excommunicated. The laity was expected to accept doctrines ecclesiastical authorities taught, but the operating religion became increasingly one of ritual, dependence upon saints and the Virgin Mary, and reliance upon the Church for release from post mortem discipline and sufferings and for participation in the joys of Paradise. Society had not become a theocracy, but the Roman Catholic Church had become the treasure house of truth, the conserver of religion, the arbiter of morals, and the co-partner with the State in maintaining a social order in which freedom in belief and conduct was limited by coercion. Christianity became a very humanly enforced orthodoxy in the pattern of imperialism supplemented by medieval folk-practices and superstition.

V

The Christians' share in the shaping of Christianity is to be seen in this orthodoxy. Christian groups

39

have used the political practices and theories of their members in shaping their doctrine. The relations of man and God have been described in patterns derived from the organization of states to which Christians have belonged. Indeed, orthodoxy might be described as transcendentalized politics. While theologians have justified dogmas by philosophy, they have always assumed that the revelation upon which their systems have been based is consistent with some social or political practice with which they were acquainted and which they treated as unquestionable. The authors of Protestant Confessions, like the organizers of the Roman and Eastern Catholic Churches, had no experience in democracy. They all lived under some type of unconstitutional, often absolute, monarchy, in which subjects had no rights opposed to the power of the sovereign. Theologians had no difficulty, therefore, in interpreting the Biblical material which embodied divine revelation, for it, too, reflected the experience of people who knew nothing of democracy. As a sovereign, God gave commandments to the first man, Adam, who promptly became disobedient. As a result, he was punished, and since he was the ancestor of the race, the whole race shared in his guilt and corruption of nature which resulted from his disobedience. But God gave laws to a chosen race, the Hebrews, by which they might win and enjoy his favor. It was a contract into which he entered with humanity. But neither this race nor the world to which the divine law was tentatively extended were obedient. Their corruption of nature made such obedience impossible. God, however, either because he was merciful, or, as many of the older church fathers claimed, because he wished to fill up the ranks of the angels which had been depleted by the revolt of Satan and his party, determined to select certain persons from this damned humanity to share in the bliss of heaven. So God in the second person of the Trinity became incarnate in the Virgin Mary, and a new contract was made that those who would accept Jesus as the Son of God and judge of the world would be saved. The question as to whether any persons besides the elect would have the ability to make such a decision was answered in a variety of ways, but generally in the negative, although the sad consequence of this inability was not to be disclosed until the Day of Judgment. Then the non-elect would find themselves in the torture chamber in Hell under the charge of Satan. The act of grace on the part of God, however, needed some justification, and Christ by dying satisfied the injured dignity or the justice of the sovereign God. Feudal practices are here obvious patterns of doctrine.

This political scenario can be found in all orthodox theologies. Today the pattern is obviously anachronistic, but by it, Christians of a certain stage of political and economic development conceived of the relation of men and God, and the presence of divine love in human history. Churches became the agency by which God made known his saving love to the world. At this point, the political and juridical pattern was supplemented by practices taken over from the mystery religions, and the sacraments became the means by which the grace of God was extended to humanity.

VI

It was in accord with social process that Christianity should be still further reshaped as nationalist states developed in western Europe. Especially in those political units whose cultural life and traditions were not rooted in the Roman Empire, did this new nationalism involve a break with the imperial papacy and the Holy Roman Empire of the Hapsburgs. The rise of Protestantism was a phase of this disintegration of the imperial idea. Each state in the territory lying outside the area of the old Western Empire developed its own church. The religion of a government became the religion of its people. Within the area of the Western Empire, this revolution was crushed by those whose political and economic interests were identified with those of the Roman Church, but in various German states, in Scandinavia, in England, Scotland, and Wales, national churches were established which were supported by the state. Catholic Church unity gave way wherever Protestants organized churches. Inherited Christian doctrines that could not be supported by appeal to Scripture were rejected. The naïveté with which the Reformers claimed to rely only on biblical revelation was equaled by their readiness to accept doctrinal interpretations given Scripture by councils and church Fathers.

Within the Protestant movement, there were two streams. Calvinism was organized in municipalities by those who were already sharing in the new commercial and industrial activity from which modern capitalism developed. On the other hand, among the states of the German princes who followed Luther, no such economic development was marked. The Lutheran churches represented a social order largely unaffected by the democratic tendencies of the bourgeois movement which Calvinism expressed. The various Confessions of Protestant churches were drawn up by political bodies and were intended to preserve the solidarity of state-supported churches, all of which preserved political practices.

The extent to which anti-imperialism affected these churches varied as new groups arose in a social order. They grew democratic where the bourgeois class became influential. The struggles between the European states were given a religious character which sanctified a brutality which would be incredible were it not true that brutality and terrorism have always been the agents of idealists who get control of military power. By the seventeenth century the struggle between the new conception of the absolute monarchy by divine right and constitutional

43

monarchy became acute in England. At the same
time there developed groups of Christians who
sought to withdraw from the state church and organize independent churches. Such a movement embodied the rising bourgeois democracy. It was opposed
to anything that savored of the papacy. These non-
conformist bodies rejected episcopacy and sacramen-
talism. Subjected to persecution, especially during
the period of the Stuarts, they sought safety in America, where they founded scattered colonies. There
came also to America persecuted minorities of other
states, as well as those who wished to exploit the economic possibilities of the new continent. With few
exceptions, these immigrant churches were Calvinist.
Their members came from the bourgeois class of
Europe and expressed in the organization of their
churches the democracy which was to condition the
development of western culture for succeeding centuries. In some cases they set up short-lived theocra-
cies. In many of the colonies churches were supported by the state. But these conditions soon became
impracticable because of the increase in population,
and Protestant churches became institutions within a
bourgeois social order, ministering to a religious experience centered upon salvation from a realistic
hell, the maintenance of acquired rights and individual respectability. Churches became less channels of
grace and guardians of doctrine, and more censors
of individual behavior. Their sense of religious function was limited by their members' participation in

democratic individualism which sought to acquire and maintain rights by abolishing privileges.

Religious liberty can be said to have been no more theoretically absolute in these colonies than in the rest of Christendom, but this variety of church organization and the absence of state control prevented the establishment of any state-supported church when the colonies finally organized the federal government of the United States. The importance of the first amendment to the federal constitution, with its establishment of religious liberty so far as the federal government is concerned, may be said to be epoch-making. At the time, no such condition existed in any of the European countries, either Catholic or Protestant. There was some degree of religious tolerance in Switzerland and Holland, but acceptance of churches as non-political units and the right of people to organize themselves religiously as they saw fit were the contribution of America. Religious liberty came by the way of ecclesiastical variety. Denominations arose as free religious groups preserved elements of state-supported churches or, as in the case of the Baptists and Methodists, organized religious movements, which did not spring from state churches. Democracy and religious liberty were thus inseparable in origin and inseparable in history.

It was natural for local immigrant churches to group themselves for purposes of co-operation in accordance with the forms with which they were acquainted. This was especially true of Presbyterian, Episcopalian, and Lutheran bodies. Radically democratic and independent bodies like the Baptists were at first suspicious of any sort of union, for fear of some type of authority. With them each congregation was self-administering and altogether independent. But in the course of time they yielded to the trend towards association for practical purposes, particularly the organization of new churches and the conduct of missions. At the present time they are bound together loosely in nation-wide conventions which have no theological authority but are intended primarily for the accomplishment of various tasks in the field of missions, evangelization, publication, and religious education. There has grown up among them, therefore, a feeling of denominational unity which, however, has no formal theological basis.

VII

In recent years differentiation within the Christian movement has been offset by a tendency towards re-integration. Such a tendency is the natural accompaniment of the collectivism to be seen in combinations of capital and unions of labor within the economic field. At first this was limited to membership of individuals in interdenominational organizations like the Evangelical Alliance, Young Men's and Young Women's Christian Associations, and Sunday School Associations, but as democratic principles

became socialized and applied to groups, co-operation among Christian bodies has become an increasing element of Christianity. Speaking generally,
it follows two courses; that towards Catholic unity
carrying forward the imperialistic trend, and that
towards federation expressing the democratic tendency to co-operate in common tasks.

The desire for Catholic unity rests on the pre-
sumption that there is a supernatural body known as
"the Church" from which no division in religious
organization is permissible. Among Protestant
churches such a conception does not imply the recognition of the Papacy, but a proposal that a basis of
unity can be found in the acceptance by a church of
the Nicene creed, of the sacraments, and of a group
of ministers whose special duty would be the administration of the sacraments. This attempt at unity
has naturally been ignored by the Roman Catholic
Church, but it has been favored by the orthodox
churches of continental Europe and the Near East.
Under the influence of its leaders two conferences
on Christian Faith and Order have been held. The
second, held in Edinburgh in 1937, issued a general
statement little affected by the trend of Christian development in democracies.

The federative movement expresses the growing
recognition that democracy must include groups as
well as individuals. The Federal Council of the
Churches of Christ in America is the outstanding il-
lustration of this tendency. It rests upon the basic

conviction that groups of different origin and different theological formulas can express their common function in facing tasks co-operatively. Such a federative movement differs from a search for unity on the basis of some ecumenical creed, although only evangelical denominations are as yet represented in the Federal Council. A more organic conception of the relations of denominations is to be seen in the United Church of Canada, where Methodists, Congregationalists, and a majority of the Presbyterians combined in a new organization in which theological differences of the older sort were waived, and methods of church organization were combined in a self-controlled church body. Altogether, it is clear that Protestant churches are attempting to counteract the excessive individualism of a pioneering period. We may still expect to see in democratic countries the emergence of sects, but we may also expect to see the elimination of religious bodies that no longer serve the purpose for which they were organized. Protestant denominations seem to be grouping themselves in accordance with the social experience which furnishes their techniques for expressing the common function of Christian bodies. In statements of what these Protestant groups regard as basic doctrine, it would be difficult to find radical differences. Denominations have become less consciously theological mobilizations and more frankly organizations for fulfilling their function to satisfy religious needs. So far as democratic society is concerned, the one certain way for Christians to get together is to work together.

The effort to develop an ecumenical Christianity embracing both Catholic and Protestant churches is halted not so much by theological and Christological beliefs as by the contrast between the imperial and the democratic social orders embodied in the two types of church organization.

VIII

While the vast majority of Christian churches hold to essentially the same beliefs, a genuinely ecumenical theology is impracticable. The inspiration and authority of the Bible, the Trinity, the divine incarnation through the virgin birth, the resurrection of Christ, a corrupt and guilty human nature from which individuals can be saved only by a divine act, the reconciliation between man and God by the atoning death of Christ, and immortality with rewards and punishments, are elements in Catholicism and Protestantism alike; but the organization of such beliefs when viewed historically is seen to be the successive rationalizations of function reflecting social conditions in which various churches have developed. Such a process has been genetic and pragmatic. Changes have been always within the limit of the religious inheritance of Christian groups, and have persisted because they have therefore been given authority. Where no changes in social orders have

49

occurred, doctrinal orthodoxy has been static. Where cultural changes have been opposed and churches have held tenaciously to religious inheritances born of an outmoded past, the maladjustment of groups develops into a struggle between social reorganization and religion itself. Such antagonism is particularly marked in non-Protestant countries, but it is to be seen also in church bodies that have maintained the authority of seventeenth-century theology. In democratic social orders, Christian groups tend to readjust their religious inheritances to conditions which are transforming group relations in the cultural, economic, and political environment. In some cases, this has resulted in the organization of Christian groups which cut loose from orthodoxy.

So long as different Christian groups are composed of persons living in different social orders and subject to different social pressures, social minds, cultural interests and scientific and social ideologies, they will have their own theologies. It could not be expected that churches with the historical, social, and political background of Greek orthodoxy should have the same theological interests and ecclesiastical structure as those that have developed within the political and economic environment of a democracy. The doctrines which have been carried along by such groups will be questioned and revalued in the same proportion as they respond to the influences of other groups.

The same is true of the content given those beliefs which have come to be accepted by most Christians.No one of them was ever treated as subject to unchanging definition. Even when such definition was given by authority, it has been re-explained by theologians and ecclesiastical bodies to meet new intellectual and social tensions. The recent effort at such revaluation, commonly known as modernism, has been driven out of sight by ecclesiastical authority in Roman Catholicism, but it has reappeared in every land where the spirit of democracy guarantees religious freedom. In such a process there already is a liquidation of doctrines. The accumulation of formulas reached in the sixteenth and seventeenth centuries by national churches is being dissolved as they are seen to be the utilization of patterns drawn from outgrown social experience. But the function of churches which the theologies of the past have expressed is being re-expressed gradually by groups both within and without the existing churches in techniques and formulas characterizing social orders with which they co-operate.

IX

To insist upon formulas which do not represent the religious situation and experience of groups in touch with modern conditions of social process violates the general law of group relationships. Imperialism and democracy are still struggling for the direction of Christianity. In more specific terms, European and American conceptions of the Christian religion and its relationship to social process must come to terms. In speaking of "the Church," American Christians have not sufficiently championed the contribution which America has made to the development of the Christian religion. Continental European churches have had little or no experience in democracy, and have too little respect for religious minorities within a state. Co-operation with such churches is highly desirable but American Christianity with its achievement of co-operation through federation finds itself opposed by the imperialistic conception of a Catholic Church which looks at denominations and sects as divisive and heretical. The basic difference between the two movements has been obscured by vocabularies, but it still exists. In co-operation with all types of Christian organizations, American Christians, by reason of their experience of federation in politics and in religion, can forward a Christian morality and religion which is not limited by presuppositions derived from the Roman empire and medieval culture. In so doing, they will guarantee the future of Christianity as a religious movement prolific in groups having the same function, but differing in structure and formula. From the days of Paul, there has been such variation. Catholic unity has existed only when variant groups have been crushed.

A genuine ecumenicity consists in the identity of function of all churches. In the light of history and therefore in a non-catholic sense, we can use "the Church" as the generic term for variant groups making faith in Jesus Christ the means of participation in the personality producing activities of the universe.

4

THE CHRIST
OF THE CHURCHES

A RELIGION IS AS TRULY
the work of its adherents as of its founder. Christianity, as we inherit it, is far enough from the teaching of Jesus. The glorious cataclysm which he and his immediate followers expected, never occurred. The company of enthusiastic believers in its coming was replaced by a continuous group involved in social process. The Christ of "the Church" is the Christ of the gospels reinterpreted by Christians. To extend his ministration to individuals and groups has been the function of the churches. The continuity of this group belief has been threatened by changes in personnel and social processes; it has gained new content from religious practices; its philosophical and theological basis has repeatedly been challenged by new habits of thought; but thanks to group solidarity, the Christian religion as a form of social behavior making faith in Jesus central has bred true to itself.

This loyalty has given content to Christianity and distinguishes it from other religions. As groups of

Buddhists embody loyalty to Gautama, and groups
of Moslems to Mohammed, so Christians are loyal
to their conceptions of Jesus.

I

This loyalty has always been subject to redefinition. In the beginning, the interpretation given Jesus
was that of the Jewish revolutionary psychology
which we know as the Messianic hope. His first followers regarded him as the one whom God had empowered to bring about the deliverance of the Jewish people from foreign control, defeat Satan the
prince of the age, and punish, or to use a modern
term, liquidate those who had subjected God's people to ignominy and suffering. They were not interested in social or political reform, but in a divinely
instituted catastrophe. But they did not forget that
to prepare for the coming Kingdom of God, Jesus
had relied upon love rather than violence. That
thought of the latter was with him is to be seen in
the story of the Temptation, and in his directions
to his disciples to sell their coats and buy swords;
but in the end, he did not permit violence, even in
defense of his own safety. Rather than doubt the
supremacy of love, he submitted to arrest and, paradoxically, was crucified as a revolutionist, the King
of the Jews.

It is a tribute to the influence of his personality
that the group that had gathered around him in the

expectation that he would restore the kingdom to Israel did not lose faith on account of this defeat. On the contrary, they believed that he had risen from the abode of the dead, gone to heaven, and would return to carry out his Messianic office during their own lifetime. But this triumphant Lamb of God was to be the Lion of the Tribe of Judah, and pictures of his victory as set forth in the Apocalypse, which became one of the sacred books of Western Christians, were as sanguinary as the most violent of the revolutionists could have desired. But even such expectations did not make Jesus other than the revealer of the love of God. It was the content of love that was not understood.

II

The change of personnel in the Christian groups from Jews to non-Jews inevitably involved a change in the inherited beliefs and social tensions, but there was no lessening of the interest in the supernatural element. The Day of Judgment stretched across the future. Salvation consisted in acquittal by the Judge. The transformation of life from mortality and the resurrection from the dead were due to supernatural power conditioned upon belief in the historic Christ as an emergence of the divine in humanity. The change of the Christian movement from Jewish to Gentile did not threaten any of these elements. It rather led to a revaluation of the significance of

Jesus from the point of view of Greco-Roman culture. The original Messianic definition involved no
peculiarity in his birth but rather the impartation to
him of the divine spirit which enabled him to do
more than was possible for other men and to become the first fruits of all those who were to share
in the higher personal life of the coming kingdom
of God. But such a conception of his superhuman significance needed to be re-stated to have full meaning
for the non-Jewish mind. The Messianic vocabulary
and expectations were retained but revalued.

The beginning of the rationalizing of the supernatural Christ is to be seen in Paul. "Christ" becomes hardly more than a name and the non-Jewish
term "Lord" takes its place as a religious description. As the churches developed there was a natural tendency for those Christians who were affected
by current theosophical and gnostic thought to place
the Lord Jesus in some current schema of supernatural beings. The reaction of Paul to this tendency is
plain. When first he was confronted with the intellectual habits of the Hellenistic world he bitterly opposed "the wisdom of this age" and insisted upon the
simplicity of the Messianic valuation of Jesus. He
had, so he told the Corinthians, a wisdom which was
not that of philosophy but of the Spirit. This philosophy, however, he does not think his readers are
capable of understanding and so he does not disclose
it. The gospel which they believed was simple, one
of historical facts which by a new interpretation of

prophetic passages declared Jesus to be the Messiah. To go beyond it was to enter the field of ethics. Philosophy puffed up but love built up. The apostle found the churches of Asia Minor, always a hotbed of extravagant religious teachings, confronted by the effort to locate Jesus in a theosophical hierarchy of supernatural beings. Paul's treatment of such a trend was non-argumentative. He had already conceived of the Christ as pre-existent, although he had never really systematized that conception with his Jewish belief as to the Spirit of God. It had been enough for him to say that the Lord was the Spirit. There he wished the matter to rest. Appealing as he did to Christians who were singularly susceptible to contemporary supernaturalism he does not undertake to disprove the existence of other heavenly beings, but he asserts that they were all included in his conception of Christ. By such a rough and ready avoidance of discussion so attractive to the Greco-Roman mind, Paul centers attention upon the moral significance of the new life which had been conferred upon those who had accepted Jesus as Lord. Love was to be the supreme motive with them as it has been with Jesus, who had descended from heaven to reconcile men with God.

III

The revaluation of the Messianic significance of Jesus was carried forward in the Johannine literature. The Fourth Gospel was written for a second or third generation of Christians who were unacquainted with Palestine and Jewish customs. They had taken over the Messianic interpretation of Jesus only to find that the expectation of the original disciples had not been fulfilled. In consequence, their faith needed to be confirmed. To accomplish this, the author translates the idea of the Kingdom of God, the Messianic Judgment, the resurrection and the return of Jesus into thought-forms more intelligible to non-Jewish Christians. The interpretation given Jesus as the Logos made flesh is not explicitly carried forward in the gospel; but Jesus is always represented as a superhuman person, one with God, who with the Father can come into human experience, and give his followers the superhuman life of the coming Age—eternal life—which is superior to Satan, sin, and death.

In this revaluation, the historic Jesus already given Messianic value in the Synoptic Gospels and the nature of a heavenly being in the Pauline preaching, is seen as a divine being, already an object of worship. The Messianic office, with its eschatalogical salvation, is not denied; but it is subordinated to the spiritual life of the believer. Material was thus provided which in later theological controversy was to serve to justify the worship of Jesus as the incarnate Logos, who created the world, who partook of the divine nature, and was the light which streams upon every person born into the world.

Such a historical approach to the Christ of the Church is not to be confounded with the so-called symbolical criticism of W. B. Smith. According to this view, Israel is the Son of God. The Jesus of the Gospels is a pre-Christian god, the personified symbol of the people of Israel, who had been crucified as a nation by Roman imperialism, but through its projection of its monotheism into the Hellenistic world, was to gain spiritual headship of humanity.

While it must be admitted that the Gospels include material of later Christian faith, any such interpretation of the position given Jesus by the Christian community is ingenious rather than historical. The true approach is through the revolutionary psychology of the Messianic hope. The belief that God would empower some person with his Spirit to become a savior of his chosen people was the compensatory interpretation of the subjection of Israel to the pagan masters. A pre-Christian Christ who was a god is quite beyond discovery by any sober methodology.

The practices and attitudes of Christian groups lie back of the discussions as to the relation of the Son with the Father. A practice that has once become thoroughly embedded in the subconsciousness of a group may require a philosophy to rationalize it, but it has final authority. Within original Jewish circles, to speak of Jesus as the Son of God was to paraphrase a Messianic interpretation; but to the Hellenistic mind, the term was not official, but personal.

Those accustomed to unphilosophical polytheism found no difficulty in worshiping Jesus, in praying to him as a god, and in seeking union with him in the way of the mystery religions. Ignatius, though speaking of God and Jesus Christ, does not hesitate to refer to Jesus as "our inseparable life, the will of the Father"; of "the blood of God"; and of the prophets as being saved through union with Jesus Christ. He glorifies "God even Jesus Christ." "Wherever Jesus Christ is, there is the Catholic Church." Such expressions, however, no more repudiated monotheism than does the custom of evangelical preachers today to address prayer to Jesus. They vocalized group practices born of a belief that Jesus was empowered by the resident Spirit of God to be a savior.

IV

It is from such a point of view that one must examine the theological discussions of the third and fourth centuries. Political situations prevented the extension of love beyond individual morality. The one free area was philosophical speculation.

Monotheism was supported both by the Hebrew Bible and the Hellenistic philosophy. The early Christian apologists were indifferent to the tendency among philosophically minded people to regard the various divinities as names for one single god, and preferred to die rather than even formally to burn incense before idols and the statues of the emperor.

Monotheism and worship of Jesus as God had to be harmonized.

By the second century, the attention of Christian thinkers was centered upon the adjustment of the belief in a supernatural quality of Jesus with a metaphysical theism. The events of Jesus' life were given a supernatural coloring by the redefinition of the "Son of God" in terms of a virgin birth. The question of his nature and relation to God the Father became of supreme importance. The search for truth overshadowed the extension of love.

There were two patterns in which the treatment of Jesus as God was justified. One was that of current cosmology, which claimed to have wisdom, or gnosis. This type of philosophy was older than Christianity, and made a decided appeal to the Hellenistic mind. Under its influence many Christians found intellectual guidance. It is too elaborate for exposition here, but its pattern is plain. At the one extreme, was posited an unknowable principle from whom, in a series of supernatural marriages, there emerged various superhuman beings called Aeons, which in turn, finally got in touch with evil matter. One of them became incarnate in Jesus. The extraordinary volume of Irenaeus *On Heresies* plunges one into an interminable and all but unintelligible exposition of what seems absurdity; but, properly estimated, these Gnostic writers were really engaged in a pre-scientific intellectual process akin to philosophical evolution. If they had been successful, Christianity would have been submerged under a metaphysical, or rather theosophical, system from which it probably never would have emerged.

That such a fate did not befall the young religion is due to the triumph of those Christian groups which based their belief on an authoritative collection of Christian writings. Tertullian, in his treatise *On the Prescription of Heretics,* refuses heretics, that is to say, the scientific-religious thinkers, the right to argue on the basis of their claim to be seeking new truth. He protests that they have no need of new truth. "Away with attempts," he cries, "to produce a mottled Christianity of Stoic, Platonic, and dialectic conception. We want no curious disputation after possessing Jesus Christ, after enjoying the Gospel. With our faith, we desire no further faith, for this is our basic faith: that there is nothing which we ought to believe besides."

The solidarity of Christian groups relying upon history saved Christianity from disappearing in contemporary theosophy, but the danger of its lapsing into polytheism because of its worship of a historical character was none the less pressing. And it was Tertullian who developed the second pattern which was to become the basis of the Christian doctrine of God and its Christology. As a lawyer, he knew that the same person could appear in different "personae," or capacities, in different courts. He could, for instance, have a case in one court in which he was a creditor, and a case in another court in which he was a debtor.

He was the same man, but there were two legal "personae." This analogy Tertullian applied to theology. The metaphysical conception of substance common to the thinkers of the time, was naturally extended to God. The divine substance or essence appeared in three "personae"; the Father, who was the Creator, the Son, who was incarnate in Jesus the Savior, and the Holy Spirit. Such a presentation was really metaphorical, but later became metaphysical. Was the Son really of the same substance as the Father, or was he a supreme being created by the Father?

Anyone familiar with the theological discussions of the third and fourth centuries knows that they were concerned with something more than, as Carlyle says, "a diphthong." The real issue was one between monotheism and polytheism. Were Christians in the Christ they worshiped to have a God who, however unique, was not divine in the sense of being of the same substance as God the Father? It would be a mistake to identify Arianism with modern Unitarianism; for the Jesus whom Arius would worship was neither man nor angel, but a being who was next to God the Father, who fulfilled the functions of a real God but was of only "like" substance. It should be borne in mind that in the Greco-Roman world, polytheism was endemic. The philosophical struggles which the Christian religion reflects were fundamental to a religious conception of the relation of man and the deity. When, at Nicea, the fathers of the Church voted that the Son was of the same di-

vine substance as that of God the Father, a metaphor which was entirely intelligible was erected into
a metaphysic which made Jesus a problem to be
solved only by authority. For it was inevitable that
the question would arise as to whether he had a human nature as well as divine nature, and if so, what
relationship the two would have in the historic character. Students of Church history will recall the bit-
terness and the brutality of the struggle which
marked the discussion of this problem of transcen-
dental psychology. As a matter of fact, it never was
settled; but in the Council of Chalcedon, the bare
facts were stated that, in his human nature, Jesus
was the same substance as mankind, and in his divine
nature, the same substance as God the Father, and
that he had one personality. But the Creed does not
state how that personality was formed, or whether
each nature or the historic personality had a will.
Every attempt at finding a solution to such problems
was condemned and Christians fell into groups
whose chief characteristics were quarrelsomeness in
the name of some slogan like "one nature," "one
will."

Though the Christ of the ecumenical Creeds is a
different person from the Messiah of the Gospels,
the religious faith of the Jew in one empowered by
the Holy Spirit to be a Savior, found parallel expression in the vocabulary and pattern of the in-
quisitive and argumentative theologians and councils of the Greco-Roman world. Such patterns and

beliefs became orthodoxy because Councils, by some form of coercion, made essential to salvation the acceptance of both the Messianic belief found in the so-called Apostles' Creed, and the Greco-Roman metaphysical analysis found in the ecumenical Christology.

But Christians have not always been content to leave the doctrine of Christ in the unexplained realism of Chalcedon. There have been repeated attempts to solve the problem of how the two natures could be combined, the most important of which was seen in the Adoptionist controversy, which was, in effect, the effort of various Christian groups to substitute the Messianic interpretation of Jesus found in the Synoptic Gospels for the Christology of orthodoxy. But successive Councils refused any such reversion, and the figure of the Christ, with one personality and two natures, persists to this day.

Further, the early churches judged it imperative to recognize the human nature of Christ because salvation involved the sacrament of the Lord's Supper. In that meal the believer was convinced that he partook of the body of Christ. The flesh as well as the spirit had to be saved if the Savior was to bring a completed immortality. If the body of Christ, as Docetic teachers insisted, was only a phantasm and the divine substance had never been in actual touch with matter; if in the incarnation there were two natures and two wills, and so a duality rather than a real personality; if as Apollinaris insisted the Eter-

nal Son took the place of the rational mind of the
human nature; if the two natures were, as it were,
amalgamated into something which was neither, then
the practices of the church were themselves unjusti-
fiable. The fact that Councils could not find any
formula satisfactory to the various theological
schools did not affect popular Christianity. The
formulas which the Councils finally did select were
the outcome of a determination to maintain the in-
tegrity, solidarity and practices of Christian groups
whose function was fundamentally religious.

In disregard of this fact, some attempt has been
made to explain the Nicean formula by way of psy-
choanalysis. Such interpretation claims that while
Christianity was the religion of a depressed group,
there developed antagonism to father-authority (a
most important element in the psychoanalyst's interpretation of religion). Jesus the Son was put in the
place of the Father, and there thus developed the
compensatory belief that man could become God.
When Christianity became the religion of the rulers
rather than of the depressed class, a radical difference was found between the god-substance and man-
substance. Man never could become god. Depressed
and suffering humanity was to rest content with the
hope of joys in heaven after death.

That there is some truth in such a psychoanalyti-
cal reading of doctrinal history cannot be denied,
but it would be impossible to show that faith in the
Son of God ever involved the belief that men could

become God. The interpretation given Jesus when Christianity was the religion of an extra-legal but not necessarily depressed class, never involved the apotheosis of a historical person. Jesus was worshiped, not as a man who had become a god, but as a man into whom God had come. The interpretation which Jesus gave God came from filial rather than parental experience, and so became a type of new brotherhood composed of those into whose lives God had also come. The community of experience expressed in the Christian group was not that of humanity becoming God, but of human nature transformed by contact with God. From this came emancipation from sin and from death.

v

The decisions of councils in expressing the function of a church became the substance of an implicit faith on the part of Christians. It was not necessary for lay piety to find answers to the problems with which the clergy were concerned. It was enough for them to perform the required ritual acts, pray for mercy, repent and confess their sins to the priest, receive absolution from the church, perform such works of penance as would give them merit in the courts of Heaven, bespeak the assistance of the Virgin Mary and the saints, and above all, accept the salvation from divine wrath which had been brought by the Son of God. For purposes of religious instruction, the share of Jesus in producing the forgiveness of God was pictured in social patterns expanded into mythologies. He was a ransom paid to Satan, who was in charge of the underworld of the dead. In exchange for him, Satan let the Biblical saints who had died before the incarnation escape to Heaven. By virtue of his divine nature, of which Satan had been unaware, Jesus was able on the third day to arise from the abode of the dead, leaving Satan outwitted.

The morality of this procedure is certainly questionable, and it never became more than a homiletical device. The need of a dogma as to the atonement was hardly felt by the Catholic theologians since the sacrifice of Jesus was re-enacted in the ritual of the mass. The atoning significance of the death of Christ found its way into theology, one might say, by indirection.

In the eleventh century, the acute mind of Anselm, in order to convince Jews and infidels as to the need of an incarnation of God, turned to the political practices of the day. How could God the Father pardon sinners and admit them into the company of the angels, and at the same time preserve that dignity which the feudal system presupposed? The answer of Anselm gave a new element to orthodox Christology. God became incarnate in order to produce one who, because sinless and human could make satisfaction for the injury done the dignity of God made by sinful humanity. Thus, in his effort to show why God became man by appeal to social habits rather than to revelation Anselm developed a new doctrine of the Atonement.

And this conception of the death of Christ was preserved by Protestantism even when the Roman Catholic doctrine of transubstantiation was abandoned and faith made the sole basis for the enjoyment of the salvation which the atonement of Christ had made. An acquaintance with the theology of Calvinism will show how Christ was pictured as a sacrifice that not only appeased the wrath of God, but also satisfied his justice. The theological pattern was that of law as chiefly concerned with punitive justice. The Protestant penitent as truly as the Catholic penitent pleads the sufferings of Christ as having been incurred for him. One has only to recall hymns which we still sing, to appreciate this fact.

This conception of the atoning Christ is still dominant in the formulas and preaching of most evangelical churches. It is too easily pictured to be abandoned. But there has been a softening of many of its details.

By the end of the revolutionary period of the eighteenth and early nineteenth centuries, the political and social presuppositions which underlay the orthodox doctrines of salvation were replaced by newer presuppositions born of the rise of democracy. Under orthodoxy, humanity had no rights, and was wholly at the mercy of God, who might or might not, as he saw fit, select individuals for eternal blessedness. Deism, by transferring some of God's activities to Nature, had made such sovereignty more like that of the Parliamentary government of England, but the Unitarian movement in the spirit of democracy insisted that man had rights and that God had duties. This naturally affected its view of Christ. He became less an atoning sacrifice than an example of the divine life in humanity. This in turn led to a denial of the Nicean formula as to his deity.

VI

New influences were still to come as the historical method was extended to the study of the New Testament. On the one side there is the extreme position of those who, like Drews, would deny the historicity of Jesus and see in Christ a hypothetical God. This movement has been so thoroughly discredited by the historians that it needs only to be mentioned. On the other hand, the sober application of the historical method to the Gospels as the outgrowth of the life of the churches, and especially research in the relationship of Christianity to contemporary religious movements in the Greco-Roman world, have given Jesus new importance in our modern world. In so doing, it has passed from metaphysics to morality. But this shift of interest raises old questions in new forms. Was Jesus a victim of circumstance, or did he, in his own social situation, and by the use of contemporary vocabularies and concepts, really embody the ideal of what life would be if properly adjusted to God? Such questions can not be answered by doctrines shaped in patterns of begetting, virgin birth, vicarious atonement, and Hellenistic metaphysics. They are moral rather than speculative. Questions which concerned ancient Christians debarred from political and social reform, are very different from those propounded by concern as to a social order. In the ecumenical creeds, there is no trace of interest in morality beyond the belief in the forgiveness of sins. They have never prevented churches and individuals from being controlled by contemporary habits and standards of conduct. This is deplorable, but it is also understandable. The center of a group's interest will become that of its constituent individuals. So long as faith *about* Jesus assured acquittal at the coming Judgment Day, there was little inducement to make his teachings as to love central. Logically, the acceptance of the deity of Christ should have made Christian churches the champions of his teaching and his example the basis of conduct, but from the days of Nicea, the presuppositions for Christian morality have been generally derived from a social order rather than the teachings of Jesus; even groups, which like the followers of St. Francis, undertake to reproduce his life, center attention upon his poverty and celibacy. It was not until the historical approach to the Gospels replaced the dogmatic, that the social bearing of his teachings was perceived. Jesus became a more significant element in shaping the function of the church as an amoral christology ceased to be supreme. Even those churches that preserved traditional orthodoxy have perceived that he was interested in love rather than in metaphysics, and that the ethical content of his teaching is not to be measured by the standards of Greco-Roman philosophy and seventeenth century nationalism. That the centering of ecclesiastical interest upon sacrificial morality is as yet only partial, is to be seen in the limitation of the members in the newly established World Council of Churches of those who accept Jesus as "God and Savior." Such reproduction of the ancient Catholicism may be advisable as a way of breaking down the century-long enmities of Christian groups, but it shuts out from co-operation churches that seek to perform their religious function by making the example and teaching of Jesus their final moral idealism. Such loyalty is not confined to churches. Thanks to the influence of individuals and minorities, and those who have come under their influence, it is to be found in groups devoted to social reform but who regard the supernatural metaphysics of historical Christianity as outmoded. Such influence of Jesus is one aspect of interaction of the Christian groups with others within the contemporary social order. In democratic social orders, importance of dogma has decreased as emphasis has been laid upon Jesus as a guide to morality. It is becoming increasingly clear that the significance of churches in our modern life will be determined by the extent to which their faith in Jesus leads them to persuade their members that love is a practicable basis upon which to build individual morality and social orders because God is love. So to give Jesus moral centrality is not to deny values expressed in historical orthodoxy. It is rather to interpret the function of Christian groups in patterns derived from intellectual, social, and political trends of our modern life.

In so doing there should be no neglect of the insistence of church doctrines upon love as an attribute of God. In all theories of the atonement He initiates the method of forgiveness. Men unaccustomed to such an attitude on the part of a sovereign sought to justify its morality by appeal to current practices, but love remained as the center of the gospel and the Christian's contribution to theism.

5

A CHURCH AS A CHANNEL
OF GRACE

THE RELIGIOUS FUNCTION
of a church has been usually described as the mediation of divine grace to men.

To Protestant ears, the term has an indefinite sound. The reason for this is that in the development of Protestantism, a church has had a decreasing significance. Its chief object has, on the whole, been that of giving the correct theological content to faith. Greek orthodoxy is still dominant in anachronistic churches, whether in the Balkans or in the United States. But real unity in the Christian religion does not lie in attempts to find some formula which people can accept without agreeing as to what it really means, but in the effort inaugurated at Stockholm and carried forward at Oxford to make churches an influence in society as well as in the behavior of individuals. In such interest the conception of grace is almost lacking. Emphasis is upon the duties of churches rather than their function to further contact with cosmic activity. But in so far as Protestant churches neglect this sometimes-called mystical service, they are moving away from a dominant element in the Christian movement.

I

The recognition by primitive Christian groups of their religious function was the outcome of the association of persons having the same faith in Jesus as Savior, and the same religious experience. They all had implicit faith in supernatural powers. With no interest in social reform, they not only believed that the world was coming to an end at any moment and that Jesus would put every human being on trial to settle his eternal destiny, but they also believed that they shared in the divine power which regulated the affairs of the universe. Of democracy in the modern sense of the term, there is little or no evidence in the New Testament. The officials of a church were not elected, but set apart by God through the gift of his Spirit. Even when the church at Jerusalem cast lots for the successor of Judas, the Holy Spirit was called upon to make the selection. The presence of the divine spirit was to be seen in the gift of tongues, as well as in various other gifts. In fact, if we may trust Paul, there was danger lest the churches might become eccentric. When church-members became rivals for position, Paul appealed to the operations of the supernatural power. God had set in the church apostles, prophets, teachers, workers of miracles, and glossalalia and the complementary gift of interpretation of tongues, but all were directed by the same Spirit. The hope of the resurrection of the body and the entrance into the Messianic kingdom of heaven was not based upon moral perfection, but upon the influence of the spirit of God upon the believer in Christ, the Lord who is the Spirit. Yet, while according to Paul, the spirit of God worked within the Christian community or church, its presence in the believer was not conditioned upon membership in the church. The Holy Spirit came to an individual when he accepted Jesus as the Christ, and was transformed so that he already possessed eternal life, and was free from the control of death, the penalty of sin. The ability of the Galatian Christians, for instance, to work miracles was due, not to the influence of the Church, but evidenced the certainty of acquittal at the coming Judgment. He tells the Corinthians that in eating the bread and drinking the cup of the Lord, they are passing judgment upon themselves. They are to work out their salvation with fear and trembling, because it is God working within them to do as he pleased.

The influence of the Spirit was not limited to the transformation of the persons of believers and the gift to them of new powers. It was the basis for an ethic, which, despite Paul's minimizing of philosophy, utilized a current psychology. Personality, he held, had two elements, the outer and the inner man. The outer man, however, was not merely physical, for the word flesh with him includes elements which we might speak of as survivals of animalism, hunger, sex, and pugnacity. The inner man he does not so clearly define, but apparently, it would include the powers of choice and of reason.

The struggle within the man ceased to be between the outer and the inner man, and became a struggle between the flesh and the Spirit. Over against each other were the works of the flesh, which were obviously perversions of the natural instincts and urges of man, and the fruit of the Spirit which was moral motivation.

The company of individuals thus affected by supernatural power constituted the body of Christ, contributing to its efficiency. Obviously, this conception is more than religious atomism. Historically speaking, it became the basis of a group solidarity. "The Church" which Paul describes metaphorically evidently stood generically for groups of those having the same faith in Christ and experience of the spirit. It was natural that such a conception should lead to the belief that the Christian community itself communicated supernatural influences to its members. A group always affects its members. In the case of the churches, this recognizable social law was described as grace. The personality-producing activities of the universe found expression through the group as it fulfilled its function.

II

According to ecclesiastical definition, grace is "a supernatural gift of God to intellectual creatures for their eternal salvation. Eternal salvation itself consists in heavenly bliss resulting from the intuitive knowledge of the triune God, who, to the one not endowed with grace, inhabiteth light inaccessible." Such grace may be transient help to act (actual grace) or a permanent state of grace (sanctifying grace).

Probably over no element of theology has there been more discussion. To the thoroughgoing Augustinian, salvation is due exclusively to grace. Without it, a corrupt human nature is incapable of choosing righteousness. To the Pelagian—and liberal theology is more Pelagian than Augustinian—grace is the aid given to human nature, which is not hopelessly corrupt. In current orthodoxy, as expressed in the report of the Edinburgh Conference, "when we speak of God's grace, we think of God himself as revealed in his son, Jesus Christ." God's grace is "manifest in our creation, preservation of the blessings of this life, but above all in our redemption through the life, death, and resurrection of Jesus Christ, in the sending of the holy and life-giving Spirit, in the fellowship of the Church, and in the gift of the Word and sacraments."

As stated by the Edinburgh Conference on Faith and Order the function of the Church as the body of Christ is to "glorify God in its life and worship, to proclaim the Gospel to every creature, and to build up in the fellowship and life of the spirit all believing people, of every race and nation. To this end God bestows his grace in the Church on its members through his word and sacraments, and in the abiding presence of the Holy Spirit." "The sacraments are not to be considered merely in themselves but as sacraments of the Church, which is the body of Christ. They have their significance in the continual working of the Holy Spirit, who is the life of the Church. Through the sacraments, God develops in all its members a life of perpetual communion living within its fellowship, and thus enables them to embody his will in the life of the world; but the loving-kindness of God is not to be conceived as limited by his sacraments." This last clause is a significant addition to an otherwise Catholic statement.

Whether or not those elected to salvation can choose to be lost, is a matter over which the theologians have debated. Is God's grace irresistible, or can a man choose to reject it? Can a man fall from grace, and, if so, can he be restored? All the discussions of such questions have a conditioning pattern of the divine sovereignty. God acts like the rulers with whom the theologians were acquainted. But such a basic pattern is so obviously a metaphor that it can have little weight with those who think of the Christian religion in accordance with the methods and patterns of our modern world.

For them, the function of a church involves the

cosmic order rather than a political analogy. As an atom carries electricity a religious group carries those personally responsive activities of the universe with which mankind is organically related, to which the evolution of persons is due and upon proper adjustment with which the growth of personality depends.

III

The church, as an agent in this adjustment, is a social group expressing on the level of personality the creative cosmic activity from which human personality has sprung, and with which we must be at one. If there is anything which scientists have made plain, it is that the genetic changes in nature which we call evolution are due to recombinations of existing material in response to elements of the cosmic environment. We do not know what may be the ultimate nature of matter, but we do know that electrons and protons combine in atoms, atoms in molecules, molecules in colloids, and they in organisms. But in no case does a combination modify itself in a vacuum. It reacts to and adjusts itself with elements of its environment to which older combinations did not respond. The stream of development goes on, the creative activities of the universe being seized upon and working through and with one set of combinations to produce another.

When this process reaches the level of personal

81

humanity, it does not cease. Individual persons unite in social groups, and by virtue of such co-ordination, are able to make adjustments to the universe which otherwise they would not have made. Compare, for instance, the efficiency of the adjustment to cosmic forces in the co-operative life of cities with that of primitive social orders. The particular fact with which we are now concerned is this: just as human beings, as peripatetic chemical laboratories depend upon those activities in the cosmic environment which we call chemical, so as persons they must maintain proper reciprocal relations with those personality-producing activities of the universe with which they are organically connected. Such adjustments involve social combination. Through such combinations, provided they embody the co-operative principle of love, cosmic activities reach individuals. All social combinations intended to further personal values are dynamic, but a religious group is particularly responsive to the personality-producing and personally responsive activities of the universe with which it is environed. In less oracular terms, a church as a social group will enable its members to experience God in ways not possible for unsocial individualism. Here in the evolutionary pattern is that fact which the doctrine of a church as a channel of grace embodied.

IV

A religious group is more than an aggregate of religious individuals. It has its own function to perform. It must conserve and express within itself religious emotion as well as religious conviction. Its members can share in its mediation with the divine as they co-operate in ways the group itself regards as functional. Such participation in the group's influence is made possible by worship and the sacraments.

The term "worship" is sometimes used as a synonym for prayer and communion. The confusion that results is more than verbal, for it obscures the service which participation in group action can make to the religious life. Worship is a social act. Solitariness has its religious value, for individuals have moments in which they feel detached, if not lonely, and turn for relief to whatever god they trust. But there is also a contribution to be made to individual life by sharing in the experience of others. Socialized religious emotion enriches, or at least affects, its participants. The more or less imagined radio audience is psychologically different from a congregation. For weal or woe emotions become contagious in a group. It was with true psychological insight that the early church reported Jesus as saying that he would be present wherever two or three were gathered together in his name.

The importance of an institution which can regularly organize group meetings facilitating experience of God has always been recognized. The indispensable prerequisite for its efficiency is that acts of worship be genuinely instrumental in their expression of the group's function. Usually, the patterns of worship are the extension of accustomed ways of thought and action, and consequently, much worship perpetuates the past. The ecclesiastical dress, the forms of prayer, the order of religious services, are survivals. And it cannot be denied that in a church service that carries forward an ancient ritual, there is often a solemnity which the more informal service of most Protestant churches lacks. But such experience is likely to be more aesthetic than moral. It can be felt in great cathedrals, but also in the presence of great ruins. Anachronisms have moral worth only as the emotions they arouse are in accord with the function of the group, and are directed towards action. Worship can inspire but it can never become a substitute for a sense of duty. It is cowardly to make prayer an excuse for belittling the social gospel. It is religious atavism for a congregation to beseech God for mercy as if he were an Oriental monarch or a sixteenth-century absolute king. The attempts of Protestant churches to revive medievalism in church services remind one of children playing that they are members of the court of King Arthur. If a church service is to give its participants moral strength, it must make religion less a pageant than an expression of actual life. Whatever the criticism passed on unconventional religious groups like the Salvation Army, the revival meeting, and the Oxford Group, it is undeniable that they do serve to make religion something familiar.

If a church is to appeal to intelligent persons, its worship needs to express intelligent belief. Its patterns can be drawn from biology as truly as from an Oriental state. The relations of a living organism to its environment can furnish the metaphors of religion. The S O S call over the radio means much more to the modern world than the shouting of a chieftain's name while being pursued by one's enemies. Reality always includes relationships. Organism-in-environment is a pattern in which the relationship of a man to the personality-producing activities of the universe can be made real. A group engaged in religious ceremonies can be more accurately thought of as an element in a cosmic relationship than as a group of penitent rebels seeking mercy in the courts of a king. For those who are in sympathy with scientific realism rather than ancient metaphors, worship is an experience of socialized emotion prompting to action expressing the spirit of Jesus in any relation of life. Such an emotion is a participation in those cosmic activities immanent in the group. In arousing it a church is fulfilling its function as a group among groups with other functions.

v

The normal result of such fulfillment of function is an incentive to prayer. To make a group itself an end

85

is to do violence to its function. That is a law which holds in the case of the churches. A church is an instrument rather than an end. Worship as a group action becomes individualized in prayer. Every religion illustrates this fact. Men seek help from superhuman Power in ways approved by the religion to which they belong. Prayer is universal, but not equally intelligent. It is always relative to religious conceptions, which in turn, embody patterns of social action. Where moral ideals are low, men will pray for unworthy ends. The moral significance of a prayer is that of the one by whom it is uttered.

For those who are under the influence of the scientific conception of nature, prayer to control those forces is regarded as naïve, if not superstitious. Undoubtedly much prayer must be so characterized; but for those who see in the universe activities which have resulted in human persons, such impersonal materialism is untenable. The universe cannot be detached from humanity any more than humanity can be detached from the universe. In this relationship, there must be recognition of elements in the universe which not only have co-operated in the evolution of persons, but continue in the environment with which they must be personally adjusted. As by "personal" we mean "of the order of human beings in their personal interrelations, rather than that of principal process or machine," anthropomorphism is postulated in all such relations. Human beings treat each other as persons when they attribute to physical entities met in sense-perception those self-directive and co-operative qualities which they find within themselves. Conversation is the way to a resulting adjustment.

Prayer is the utilization of such action in cosmic relations. Where a social order is based on a subject's fear of his master, prayer is likely to be a servile or unintelligent request for aid. In such prayer, the individual reproduces the patterns embodied in a religious group. This is as observable in the Christian religion as in all religions. The striking characteristic of Christian prayer is that it is limited by moral considerations. However relative to social practices has been the idealism of churches, prayer for what was regarded as wrong has never been approved by them. In the teachings of Jesus embodied in the Lord's Prayer, this is strikingly shown. Men are to pray to be forgiven as they forgive, and that this is more than a metaphor is to be seen in the explication of Jesus that unless men do forgive others, God will not forgive them.

Prayer, therefore, in the Christian sense, is neither superstitious nor magical. As human beings find fellowship through the anthropomorphism of love, so do they gain fellowship with the personality producing activities of the universe. Such anthropomorphism is not metaphysical, but instrumental. Its one indispensable requirement is that it should represent the highest moral elements expressed in a group function and in social experience. In the teachings of Jesus, this is expressed by the term "father." When in the development of the Christian religion this word became metaphysical, the conception of a sovereign that was loving as well as just became the pattern used in prayer. When this conception is weakened by the rise of democracy and individualism, it becomes almost inevitable that prayer should revert to the pattern used by Jesus as the expression of both love and control. Those who are not susceptible to metaphors, see prayer as involved in the biological fact that an organism responds to and is helped by the environment upon which it is dependent. In the case of persons such relations must be personal. But whatever conceptual medium be used, prayer becomes the means of personal adjustment to those activities of the universe which are susceptible to such personal adjustment. As the experience of centuries shows, it is the function of the church to make prayer both moral and intelligent. Other groups may lead their members to emphasize impersonal elements of the environment, but the function of the church is to stimulate prayer as a means of personal adjustment to those cosmic activities we conceive of as God.

VI

The members of a group share in its influences as they perform some act to which it gives its own significance. This fact explains the value of the sacraments. Like doctrines, they are the outgrowth of the practices maintained by the churches. The early Christian groups used a symbolical bath and a common meal. Both were derived from the practices already found in the religious groups of the Greco-Roman world, but were given particular meaning by Christians.

The bath symbolized the repentance of those whose faith in Jesus prepared them for the coming Messianic judgment. It was not long, however, before it gained new meaning. To be freed from sin infants were baptized on the basis of the faith of their sponsors, and for convenience' sake, affusion and sprinkling replaced immersion. The use of water and the baptismal formula were regarded as indispensable for baptism as an initiatory rite by which the believer was regenerated.

By the end of the first century we find Barnabas writing: "Blessed are they who, placing their trust in the cross, have gone down into the water"; and "We indeed descend into the water full of sins and defilement, but come up bearing fruit in our heart, having the fear and trust in Jesus in our spirit." Half a century or more later, we have the description of the rite of initiation as given by Justin: "They are brought by us where there is water and are regenerated in the same manner in which we were ourselves regenerated. For in the name of God the Father and Lord of the universe and of our Saviour, Jesus Christ, and of the Holy Spirit, they then receive the washing with water." A certain magical quality is attached to the use of the name of God, for Justin goes on to say that in order that the initiate "may obtain in the water the remission of sins formerly committed, there is pronounced over him who chooses to be born again, and has repented of his sins, the name of God, the Father and Lord of the universe; he who leads to the laver the person that is to be washed, calling him by this name alone. For no one can utter the name of the ineffable God. And this washing is called illumination because they who learn these things are illuminated in their understandings. And in the name of Jesus Christ who was crucified under Pontius Pilate and in the name of the Holy Ghost who through the prophets foretold all things about Jesus, he who is illuminated is washed." After this washing the initiate was brought to a meeting of the Christians where prayer was made "not only for the newly baptized person but for all Christians, that by their works they should be found good citizens and keepers of the commandments so that they may be saved with an everlasting salvation." Having ended the prayers, the Christians saluted one another with a kiss. The exposition of baptism as an expression of the new birth was carried further by the practice of touching the lips of the initiate with honey.

The importance of the common meal as a means of participating in divine power was largely due to the influence of the mystery religions. After the Christian group ceased to be Jews, its members were adults who had grown up in the religious atmosphere of the Greco-Roman world. In becoming Christians, they abandoned many of its practices, but incorporated others into Christianity. How extensive were the mystery religions can be seen in the mere catalogue of their names: those of Eleusis, Dionysus, Orpheus, Demeter, Cybele, Attis, Mithra, Isis, Hermes. But these by no means exhaust the list of the religions which moved from the East into the Roman Empire, along the lines of commerce and of the marching legions. In the mysteries, salvation from death was sought by the regeneration of believers through rites uniting them with a god who had risen from the dead. The similarity of such belief with the hope of Christianity is evident. It was natural for converts from paganism to transfer ritual significance to the practices of the churches, and the common meal of the early Christian churches became a communion with God as meals of the followers of the mystery religions were means of communion with whatever deity they worshiped. Something like this must have been in the mind of Paul when he warned the Corinthians: "You cannot drink the cup of the Lord and the cup of demons; you cannot share in the table of the Lord, and the table of demons."

This conception of the power of the sacraments has been perpetuated in all forms of Catholicism, and in Lutheranism they are co-ordinate with the Word as the agents of salvation. The dogmatic interpretation given to the sacraments, however, is really the rationalizing of the belief and practices of what might be called the working, or, as Harnack would call it, vulgar Christianity. When once a practice becomes fixed in a social group, it is all but impossible to change it. Its very antiquity gives it sanctity. It becomes the expression of a group's subconscious inheritance. The belief that men actually took the flesh and blood of Jesus into their mouths not only gave the Lord's Supper a potency of its own, but it demanded some type of miracle for its accomplishment. The dogma of transubstantiation was the outcome of this necessity. One can trace its development across a long period of Christian history. The significance of the sacraments was not born from the dogma, but the dogma was born from the practice. And the practice preserved a belief in the power to work miracles given to the Church by Christ.

Lutheranism, in modifying the current Christianity of the sixteenth century, did not undertake, as did Zwingli, to embody in Confessions only that which is positively set forth by the Scriptures. Its method, as the Confession of Augsburg shows, was not that of revolution but of reform. Those beliefs and practices could be retained which were not forbidden by the Scriptures. In consequence, the supernatural quality of the Church was abandoned with the priesthood and five of its seven sacraments. But in the case of baptism and the Lord's Supper the practices of the Christian community were too strong to permit more than a restatement of the reality of baptismal regeneration and the flesh and blood of Christ in the sacrament. No miracle was wrought. The faith of the believer was the basis of the sacrament's validity.

To the Calvinist, Christ was present spiritually in the Lord's Supper, but anything like the supernaturalism of transubstantiation and consubstantiation was abandoned. The same was true of baptism. Yet the practices themselves continued. Infants were still baptized, although regeneration was not claimed.

The development of the Protestant movement still further reduced the significance of the sacraments as possessing potency within themselves. The position of Baptists in this connection is somewhat paradoxical. On the one side, they deny any regenerating power to baptism, and yet insist that those who are not immersed are not fully observant of the Lord's command. Especially among the Southern Baptists, there is the development of an ecclesiasticism similar to that from which Catholicism emerged, for there is a very common belief in what is known as a "valid" baptism, that is to say, an immersion in the name of the Father, Son, and Holy Spirit of one who professes faith in the Father, Son, and Holy Spirit, by one who has been similarly immersed by someone who has been similarly immersed. That is to say, those who deny baptismal regeneration are at the same time insisting that there is a class of persons who alone are capable of administering "valid" baptism. Close communion naturally follows. If communion with Christ is possible only for those who have fully obeyed his commands, then it would seem that only those should be admitted to communion who have been immersed. It should be added, however, that this ecclesiastical rigidity has been modified, and in many Baptist churches it is no longer seriously stressed.

It is evident, therefore, that among Protestants the claim that any Christian is competent to come to God without any mediation of priest or Church has deprived a church of some of its strictly religious significance.

VII

But this loss of anything like magical power on the part of the sacraments does not make them any less instruments for expressing the strictly religious function of a church. You will notice that I say "a church" rather than "the church." What I have in mind is a group of Christians, whether local or denominational, which possess conscious solidarity. The sacraments as conceived by the Catholic and Lutheran stimulate religious experience and so serve as means by which the worshiper is brought into a new relationship with God through identification with a religious group. The vestigial sacraments of other churches can serve the same end. They are visible and outward signs of what has been called "a gracious spiritual transaction between Christ and believers." There are difficulties in speaking thus of a definite relationship between a human soul and a historical character of the past, and theological purists would prefer to say "gracious spiritual transaction between the worshiper and God, as conditioned by the following of Jesus." But the really significant thing is that any religious rite, if taken seriously as a dramatic confession of faith, is just as legitimate as a confession of faith in words. Protestants, especially of the uncompromising sort, are singularly neglectful of the significance of a ritual act. It is hard for them even to bend their heads, to say nothing of kneeling during prayer. Religious drama and pageants are attempts at satisfying this need of expressing dramatically religious interest, but they are apt to become entertainments which, however edifying, do not take the place of a religious cult. A Puritan ancestry makes Christians suspicious of emotionalism of any sort, unless it be singing gospel hymns. It may not be altogether fantastic to say that the singing of the inane words to be found in some of these hymns is a compensation for the neglect of the sacraments.

This psychological justification of sacraments presumes sincerity on the part of the participants, but the test of their value is not in the immediate emotion they arouse. Persons of strong imagination may be emotionally stimulated by sharing in the Eucharist, but most people who see in it a memorial meal or even an aid to spiritual communion with Christ seldom have a mystical experience. This, however, is by no means to deny value to the sacrament as a means of stimulating the religious attitude. Any rite habitually observed has its effect, and even the most non-ritualistic Protestant appreciates the value of participating in that which does set forth dramatically the fellowship of the human with the divine established by a church. To make the observance of the Lord's Supper casual or occasional, and to conduct it without due regard to the psychological value of a rite, is to detract from the significance of the group which gave it value.

For those who hold to the Catholic conception of the Church, all sacraments have a validity given them by the divinely established Church. For those Protestants who do not regard baptism as regenerating its recipient, it is an outward and visible sign of the entrance into a spiritual relationship with a Christian group. No one would say that every application of water to a person has religious value. Only as such value is given it by a religious community does it becomes baptism. The fact that in actual practice there are other methods of joining a church and so sharing in its religious life does not negate the value of the rite. If a Christian group wishes to make it the only initiation into its membership, it is acting within its rights. When, however, it asserts that it is the only way of entrance into the spiritual experiences of all Christian groups and denies the validity of such experience in the case of those who have not been baptized, it minimizes a group as a carrier of divine activity.

The religious value of the Lord's Supper is more easily seen because of its repetition. Here again, too sharp a distinction can be drawn between the Catholic and the radically Protestant positions. One may hesitate to accept the dogma of transubstantiation or any other philosophy by which belief in the real presence of the flesh and blood of Christ in the Eucharist may be justified; but one cannot deny that a church gives to the Supper a religious value, and that by sharing in it, one shares in the contributions of a Christian group to the religious life.

It is here that ecumenicity of function on the part of churches is of real value. There is inspiration in the knowledge that the local group which one enters is a part of a great community, and that its practices are recognized in a world-wide fellowship. From a psychological point of view, participation in a group experience, and the validity given to the dramatic form of such participation, presuppose a concrete group, no matter how small; but such a group will get new courage and significance as it regards itself, and is regarded by others, as an outpost of a world-wide community—a "cell" in a world-wide movement. The significance of a sacrament practiced by any local group will be increased as one sees it also practiced by innumerable other religious bodies, separated, it is true, by doctrines, forms and histories, but one in having the same function.

VIII

Since a sacrament does not have independent power in itself, but is a means of participating in the religious experience and ministration of a church, it is highly important that the conditions under which it is offered and received should be recognized as a part of the technique by which the individual is brought into relationship with the "body of Christ." The validity, that is to say, the efficiency, of baptism or the Lord's Supper is lessened in proportion as the communicant loses the sense of its symbolic value. Participation in the group experience will be proportional to the ritual attitude. Regularity demands proper administrators. The primitive Christian group had no need of priests, since it was composed of Jews who continued to worship in the Temple. The question seems to have later arisen, for we find the author of I Peter insisting that the Christians are a royal priesthood as well as an elect race and a holy nation. The acceptance of the Old Testament as a divine oracle suggested the priesthood as well as the sacrifice of Hebrew ritual. Both the Letter to the Hebrews and I Clement attempted to show that such priesthood was more than surpassed in character and services by Jesus. But in neither writing is there any intimation that there was need of a priestly order.

But the logic of the situation was unavoidable. When once the Christian community took over the pagan conceptions of the sacraments as a means of union with the divine and risen Christ, a priesthood was inevitable. A tendency in such a direction had at its disposal the embryonic government of the various churches which was regarded as the outcome of the work of the Spirit. And it was not long before the pattern of the synagogue surviving in church worship was reinforced by the administrative practices of the various religious and other groups of the Greco-Roman society. An overseer or bishop was appointed by the church itself, supposedly under divine direction. Bishops and deacons are already mentioned by Paul in his letter to the Philippians, and by the time the pastoral letters were written the office of the bishop seems to have been recognized. But even in this literature the bishop is not described as having a priestly office.

The original function of the bishop was that of administrator and guide of a Christian group. By degrees, however, as doctrinal differences began to appear among Christians, a bishop came to be regarded as possessor of the true doctrine. Ignatius insists upon this. Not only does he exhort the Ephesians "not to set ourselves in opposition to the bishop in order that we may be subject to God," but he also states that bishops are appointed by the will of Jesus Christ. A bishop who was the center of group solidarity, the repository of Christian truth and the administrator of the various rites of the churches, naturally gained priestly status. Supernaturalism, whether magical or mystical or ritual, is always administered by a priestly class. A Christian community represented supernatural power to which its members were introduced by the performance of acts given meaning by itself and administered by those whom it delegated.

Although the Catholic conception of order has been abandoned by the Protestants, their clergy can be counted upon to give religious character to funerals and weddings, make public prayers, deliver sermons, pronounce benedictions, administer baptism, and preside at the Lord's Supper. While such ministers are generally ordained by the laying on of hands by co-operating clergymen, no such signification attaches to this ceremony as in churches recognizing order. But it none the less has a meaning. The minister is the representative of a religious group. In so far, therefore, he differs from a layman, and he has duties which are determined by the function of that group. He is not a priest, but he is a minister of religion. Such a relationship makes him more than a lecturer upon morality. His supreme duty is that of leading and representing a group which furthers the personality-producing activities of the universe by making love final in all human relations.

IX

A church, therefore, does not fulfill its function if it limits its activities to the maintenance of worship and sacraments and ordained ministry. If it is in any true sense to be a channel of grace, that is if it is to bring individuals into help-gaining adjustment with the personality-producing activities of the universe, it must induce the other groups of a social order to make love—that is, recognition of personal rights—a basis for action. The language and patterns in which this conviction is aroused are of secondary importance. If fellowship between man and God is dependent upon the embodiment of love as exemplified by Jesus, it will be enough to have that love expressed. Wherever there is love, there is God. The increasing number of non-ecclesiastical groups devoted to the service of mankind are so many points of contact with those activities of the universe making towards personal values. It would not be accurate to say that humanity waits upon the action of the Christian churches for the establishment of such group media. Every religion has the same function, and every altruistic group is reinforced by cosmic activity. But such facts do not detract from the function of the Christian church. However other groups may seek to socialize reliance on love, Christian groups must fulfill their function in such social environments as they may have. They must not only furnish men of good will, but they must convince groups as well as individuals that love rather than coercion, and co-operation rather than competition, are the conditions of progressive participation in cosmic activities which are as real as gravitation or electricity. And in so doing, they themselves must mediate and socialize their own experience of such participation. This fulfillment of function, if only it becomes as widespread as churches, will make them centers of a morality that is dynamic because it is born of religious experience.

6

CHURCHES AS MORAL
FERMENTS

The history of chris-
tianity not only shows the appropriation of social
practices and trends by churches, but also the influence of Christian groups upon individuals and
groups constituting the social order. This mutual interaction is not always recognized. Particularly does
misinterpretation follow when an absolute conception of "the Church" is used as a basis of criticism
of historical churches. The failure of Christians to
exemplify absolute ideals often leads to a sense of
futility and frustration. In periods of depression,
this distrust is deepened and as among the primitive
Christians, apocalypse takes the place of process,
submission to the unknown will of God the place of
effort. God becomes almost spatially distinct from
humanity, and can be reached by no human effort.
History has no approach to a deity so conceived.
The church becomes a group of pietists waiting for
God's action, repenting of its participation in social
process and condemning the world as evil. Such pessimism, unconscious of the fact that it is itself the

outcome of political and economic collapse, ignores not only the interaction of groups, but the action of God through groups.

Indifference to history is characteristic of those, who, like theologians, do not share economic and political tensions. Accustomed to deal with abstract principles, they have neither the social experience nor the historical-mindedness to realize that just as the only democracy that ever existed is the social behavior of democrats, so the only Christianity that has ever existed is the religion of Christians. Churches in exercising their function of establishing help-gaining relationships with God through faith in Jesus Christ have always acted as elements in social process.

As has already appeared, the place which Jesus has occupied in the Christian religion has been determined by the general pattern in which the relations of man to God have been conceived, but within the limitations set by that pattern, he has been the exponent of love as a quality of the divine life. The full significance of such a belief has been imperfectly and often unintelligently seen, but it has none the less been a contribution which the Christian churches have made to social process. As the individual and society have become better understood, and the finality of a social *status quo* has been questioned, there has come a new appreciation of his teaching and example as applicable to men as well as a revelation of the character of God. New meaning is thus given to the function of the churches.

The chief interest of a group is reproduced in the attitudes of its members. Such response of individuals is more emotional than intellectual. A formula becomes a slogan. In the light of history, this fact gives pause to the centering of interest on the part of a church upon dogma. Formulas which are not basically moral, distract attention from social situations, and make church loyalty indifferent to love. Those moments in which the center of interest in church life has been doctrinal have seen the brutal persecution of heretics. Men who have believed in the deity of Jesus have not hesitated to persecute those who did not hold such a belief. One cannot look without anxiety, therefore, upon the new movement in non-Roman Catholic churches to make a belief in Jesus as "God and Savior" a basis of what they profess to be ecumenicity but which is in fact a paradoxically selective Catholicism. What the world requires of the churches is not a revival of fourth-century Christology, but the impregnation of economic and political processes with love. Only then will Jesus have given meaning to their function. If Christians are to be interested in helping make a better world, the churches must make theology secondary to morality embodying the spirit of Jesus.

I

Christians have never undertaken to put all the teaching of Jesus into operation. The fact that the churches are composed of the same persons who were engaged in the ordinary pursuits of life has made such efforts impracticable. The various societies of monks and nuns which have been so prominent in the history of Western civilization attempted to emulate the life of Jesus in certain particulars, like poverty and celibacy, but they went far beyond him in introducing ascetic practices as means of winning divine favor. The Jesus of the New Testament is anything but an ascetic. He shared in the social life of his people, dined with his friends, and encouraged his followers to believe that if they sought the divine acquittal and the Kingdom of Heaven, food and clothes would come to them. In fact, one of the charges brought against him was that he came eating and drinking, and was a friend of those who were socially condemned. His abandonment of the economic life was incidental to his organization of a community of those who awaited the end of the age and the establishment of the kingdom of God. The immediacy of cataclysm permitted no attempt at economic or political reconstruction. His directions for his followers were clearly conditioned by this eschatological expectation. To think of him as a socialist or a communist or a champion of political revolution is so unhistorical as to be special pleading. To

speak of the original group of Christians as com-
munists is likewise a misinterpretation of facts. The
pilgrims who had come to Jerusalem to celebrate the
Passover, and had there accepted Jesus as the Christ,
remained in Jerusalem, expecting momentarily the
return of the Christ from heaven and the establishment of the new kingdom. In the meantime, they had
to live. Without employment, they spent their time
in the Temple or in gatherings of their fellow-
believers. Charity became indispensable and its need
was met in the spirit of love. Enthusiasm, as well as
their fellow feeling, led to the formation of an
emergency relief fund, for sustaining unemployed
brethren. This was in no sense the establishment of
economic communism. Primitive Christians were not
producers, but consumers. In the course of a few
years they had to be supported by contributions
from the brethren of Asia Minor and Greece. Such
memories as they had of the teaching of Jesus and
his call to cheerful giving stimulated Christians to
generosity, but the church in Jerusalem neither made
charity compulsory nor organized itself as an economic society.

When groups of gentile Christians were formed
in the various cities of the Roman Empire, moral
problems at once arose. The directions given by
Paul to the Christians who had become converts
from paganism covered the full range of common
life from the length of women's hair to the purchase
of meat. They were to maintain their occupations,

and not to rely upon charity. While marriage was not desirable in view of the approaching end of the world, the apostle declared that it was not dishonorable. Chastity was a virtue based on the interpretation of the body as the temple of the Holy Spirit. Family life was to be maintained, husbands and wives being loyal to each other. In Christ they were equal, but in the family the wife was the weaker vessel. If these virtues of Christians were those of conventional morality, and their customs those of ordinary respectability, their basic motive was that which Jesus himself made central, love. This was declared by Paul to be the fruit of the Spirit. The circle of faith, religious experience, and morality was complete.

From the point of modern idealism, the omissions in the apostolic teaching are obvious. Slavery was accepted as an institution, although slaves were to be treated in a friendly way. Christians were to be obedient to government as the agent of God. The legitimacy of private property was unquestioned. The churches themselves seem to have had some disciplinary authority, for Paul refers to a case of what he regards as excessive punishment of an offender. There was, however, to be co-operation rather than coercion among the Christians, and the strong were to help bear the burdens of the weak. Suits before pagan law judges were to be avoided, Paul rather pathetically asking whether, among those who were destined to judge the angels, there could not be found some capable of settling their own quarrels.

By the end of the second century, Christian groups had developed recognizable characteristics. The *Epistle to Diognetus*, defending Christians against charges made by their opponents, describes their customs thus:

They marry, as do all (others); they beget children; but they do not destroy their offspring. They have a common table, but not a common bed. They are in the flesh, but they do not live after the flesh. They pass their days on earth, but they are citizens of heaven. They obey the prescribed laws, and at the same time surpass the laws by their lives. They love all men, and are persecuted by all. They are unknown and condemned; they are put to death, and restored to life. They are poor, yet make many rich; they are in lack of all things, and yet abound in all; they are dishonoured, and yet in their very dishonour are glorified. They are evil spoken of, and yet are justified; they are reviled and bless; they are insulted, and repay the insult with honour; they do good, yet are punished as evil-doers. When punished, they rejoice as if quickened into life; they are assailed by the Jews as foreigners, and are persecuted by the Greeks; yet those who hate them are unable to assign any reason for their hatred.

To sum up all in one word—what the soul is in the body, that are Christians in the world.

It is no wonder that a tolerant man like Pliny, who came in contact with Christians while governor of Bithynia, should have seen in the Christian movement nothing except "evidence of an absurd and extravagant superstition." From the confession of apostates he learned that Christians

met on a stated day before it was light, and addressed a form of prayer to Christ as to a divinity, binding themselves by a solemn oath, not for the purpose of any wicked design, but never to commit any fraud, theft or adultery, never to falsify their word, nor deny a trust when they should be called on to deliver it up; after which it was their custom to separate and then reassemble, to eat in common a harmless meal.

The literature of the Fathers abounds in ethical appeal and direction. The Pauline morality of dynamic spiritual freedom, however, is replaced by the legalistic morality of Judaism and the philosophical ethics of contemporary Greco-Roman life. The Christian teaching inculcated virtues to be found in the teaching of such men as Seneca, Epictetus, Marcus Aurelius, and Plutarch, but in the treatment of sex as an element in morality it made its own contribution to ethical theory.

As citizens of a heavenly kingdom living in the midst of a very earthly society, it was natural that the Christian communities should have particularly concerned themselves with sex. Such an interest has always played a part in religious movements, but Christian communties were rather unique in their opposition to the license of Greco-Roman society. Celibacy came to be regarded as especially fitting for those who wished to advance in the spiritual life. The interpretation of sex as evidence of a moral lapse was to develop under the uncompromising logic of Augustine—himself affected by his temporary acceptance of Manichaeism—into the doctrine of original sin and corruption of human nature.

The second characteristic of Christian teaching was the ethical implication of the incarnation of the Logos. For Clement of Alexandria the Logos is the "Teacher from whom all instruction comes"; "virtue is a state of the soul made harmonious by the Logos throughout the whole of life." The goal of such virtue is a blessed immortality, but there is no detail of human life without moral sanction. Dress, baths, shoes, jewelry, marriage, table manners, all are to be governed by the ideals which are involved in the belief in the Logos.

From what evidence we have, it is fair to say that these ideals were in general those of the Christian churches. That they have been taught by the moral teachers of all civilizations reaching the same degree of development as that of the Roman Empire does not lessen their significance as elements of the group pressure of churches. The highly important fact is that the Christian churches fulfilled their function in giving religious sanction to the virtues which universal human experience has recognized. Yet they did not so interpret their function as to extend the love taught by Jesus to social action. Such an idea would not be likely to occur to those living in a state where supreme political authority was vested in an Emperor rather than in citizens.

This individualist morality was to continue. After Christianity had become a licensed religion there was some rather ineffectual attempt to extend the Christian ideals into economic fields. This was particularly true of men like Chrysostom and Ambrose. In them as in many other teachers there was a tendency to recognize the monastery as the best exponent of what was regarded as the primitive communism of the Church, but their denunciation of wealth and their rhetorical appeals for embryonic socialism had no effect upon economic methods. They did, however, serve to stimulate charity.

II

Charity and social reform are two expressions of the principle of love. Charity is easier and more immediately the application of the teaching of Jesus. To give to the poor and to minister to the unfortunate are the expression of social-mindedness consistent with the maintenance of the *status quo*. Charity may not only cover a multitude of sins, but cover social inertia. If the moral significance of Jesus is limited to literal obedience to his recorded sayings, the elimination of those conditions which make charity needed would not be demanded. The directions to give to those who ask, to lend to those who would borrow, to submit to political and civil injustice, can be applicable only to those who expect the world to come to a speedy end. But thanks to the revaluation of Jesus by groups of Christians, his significance has not been limited by his words. Unconsciously, by the development of their Christology, the churches have recognized his spirit rather than his teachings. As the exponent of the saving love of God he is the inculcator of love. It has been the limitations set by culture and social patterns that have made faith in him an approach to heaven rather than an incentive to social reform.

How the Christian churches, particularly of the Eastern Empire, centered their attention upon theological orthodoxy and rested content with the conventional morality is to be seen in the centuries which followed Nicaea, and particularly after the break with the Roman church in the eleventh century. However idle speculation may be, one cannot avoid the conviction that if the Christian churches had followed the trend of the ethical interpretation of the Christian experience given by Paul and Clement of Alexandria, the disintegration of the classical civilization might have been less destructive. As it is, the failure of the churches to fulfill their religious function through the exposition of Jesus as a revealer of love, carries a definite warning to those modern Christians who would have the Church stand "over against the world" in much the same way as did the monasteries and theologians of the decadent Eastern Empire.

The Western churches were as much concerned about the nature of man as the Eastern churches were about the natures of Christ. For this interest they were largely indebted to the influence of Augustine. Thanks to him, Western theology acquired a quasi-psychological, anthropological pessimism regarding human nature. The psychological interest of Augustine was profound, but his knowledge of biology was all but lacking, and such as he had was subject to his dialectical treatment of the stories of Genesis. The result was that corruption of nature, sin and guilt became the starting point of all orthodoxy, whether Catholic or Protestant, of the Western world.

It was this which gave such great importance to divine grace, for without the power which came from God, humanity was incapable of righteousness. An unparalleled pessimism as to humanity was, therefore, offset by doctrinal regularity, piety and ritual acts. God was indeed at work in the world, but so was Satan. The kingdoms of both were in opposition to each other, and, while the generic Church represented the kingdom of God, its final triumph awaited heaven. Facing the conditions set by forces they did not originate and could not control, churches increasingly made religion a means for avoiding the post-mortem punishment due not only sins, but sin. Original sin, which every individual shared, was said to be removed by baptism; but the actual sins which were the outcome of corrupt nature deserved punishment which was inevitable except as remitted by the Church under the authorization given by Christ to Peter.

Here again the development of Christianity was influenced by practices of the churches in the Roman Empire. In the troubled days of persecutions there were always those who disavowed their faith in order to avoid suffering. When persecution ceased and churches were re-established in peace, many of these apostates sought re-admission in the interests of their eternal future. There sprang up within the Western churches two parties, one insisting that such readmission was impossible, that a church should be composed of those whose loyalty was unquestionable; and the other holding that membership in a church did not involve absolute righteousness. A church was a sort of school in morals, and so could admit to its membership those whom it sought to train in the Christian life. The latter party won, and churches became agencies for the moral development of individuals, as well as the purveyors of grace. There developed an elaborate doctrine of sin which claimed to be based upon a Christian anthropology. So far as individual Christians were concerned the practical element in this doctrine was the distinction between mortal sins, which were acts contrary to the law of God, and venial sins, which were at variance with that law but were not contrary to it. Such distinction was a corollary to the definition finally given by Thomas Aquinas: "Sin is an act not in accord with reason informed by the divine law." That is to say, it was a human act deprived of its due rectitude. But before a sin could be said to have been forgiven there was need of penance. The repentant sinner was required not only to confess, but to perform some act which guaranteed his sincerity. This practice originated in days when a definite test of the sincerity of those seeking readmission to a church was necessary, but in the course of time it became highly developed. A thoroughgoing penitential system was evolved in the churches of the British Isles, and was extended by their missionaries through western Europe. Certain acts came to have merit which could be preserved in heaven and against which the Church could, as it were, draw for the benefit of those whose sins it absolved. It is unlikely that the rank and file of individual Christians were interested in the theory which the theologians developed, but the hold of churches upon the life of Christians is evident. The sins which could be forgiven were strictly individual. Adultery, unchastity, theft, and usury were especially condemned. The Christian was supposed to confess and to get absolution for these and other sins before he could partake of the sacrament of the Lord's Supper. Thus the fear of divine punishment was a motive which worked particularly to the advantage of the Church in that it could give indulgence, that is, relief from certain forms of penance, and a mitigation of the cleansing suffering in Purgatory.

But church influence was not only negative. The constant reiteration of that for which a group stands constitutes social pressure. In the case of the churches this pressure is the outcome of function. Such virtues and duties as the Christian religion inculcates are grounded, not in an intelligent self-interest or social experience, but upon what is believed to be the will of God. The Ten Commandments are quoted in all the historic documents of Christian history as oracles but are interpreted in the light of ideas and practices with which the Christians are familiar. Such a treatment of Scripture has led to repeated renewals of legalistic morals, but the sanctions of action have been set by the churches as bodies representing the divine will. Such sanctions have been enforced by foretelling the punishment God would inflict upon those who violated His will. For centuries this punishment was described by increasingly vivid pictures of Hell. While it would be impossible to say how far this appeal to fear influenced specific moral decisions, its power to perpetuate the morality which the Church as a representative of God established, is undeniable.

As the more positive ideals for individual morality became incorporated in the church group they were extended by its members into extra-ecclesiastical relations. By the development of *mores* the original fear of divine punishment in Hell and the anxiety as to post-mortem fate lessened. Even by those who altogether abandoned the belief in Hell, and to

whom the orthodox scheme of the relations of man
and God became a homiletical scenario, these *mores*
continued to be standards of moral conduct.

The significance of a church, however, as a center
of moral influence is not thereby lost. Its primary
function still exists. It must show that morality is
grounded ultimately in mankind's relationship with
cosmic activities. A philosophy or a strictly non-
theistic ethics may support *mores* which have been
the outcome of religion, but churches are needed to
deepen the conviction that intelligent love is a practicable basis upon which to build a social order because God is love. Fear must be transformed into a
sense of the inevitable suffering attendant upon anti-
personal and anti-social acts. Men and women must
be helped to recognize the authority inherent in
man's relationship with the universe from which he
has come. Prayer must cease to be servile and become a response to and a means of personal adjustment with those activities of the universe which have
made humanity personal.

In such a maintenance of moral attitudes churches
are the chief, if not the sole, representatives of a
persistent presentation of motives which are not acquisitive. One cannot read the sermons of any period
without a new appreciation of the significance of
preaching. However the preacher may have been
subject to the cultural and other influences of his day,
and however much he may have been uncritically involved in ritual acts which sprang from popular

practices tinged with superstition, the preacher has been the mouthpiece of a social group furthering ideals which found their expression in Jesus Christ and their practicability in co-operation with God. When all allowance is made for interpretative metaphors and the too frequent hypocrisy of Christians, the influence of persistent appeal to a cosmic moral order can be traced throughout Western history. The change in social conditions, the rise of new group interests, the social problems resulting from the increase of population and the industrialization of economic life, demand the extension and implementing of these ideals by individual Christians. The self-sacrifice involved in such application of Christian principles to new conditions has too often been opposed by the official Christianity, but there have always been individual Christians who have gained new appreciation of the ethic of Jesus as an element in a church's mediation of divine influence.

To stimulate and educate individuals to make the spirit of Jesus give motive in their actions is not, however, all of the function of a church. As a group it cannot neglect the obligations which spring from its contacts with human interests. In such contacts, it must remain loyal to its own function, for a church is not an economic or a political body. Temptation has always beset a church to identify some political or economic program with the will of God, that is to say, with its own interests in such a program. True, there have been churches that have deliberately separated not only themselves, but their members, from participation in political action, but to bring man into co-operation with God by extending the spirit of love, implies a course of action clearly social. The separation of the Church and State which characterizes thoroughgoing democracies no more forbids a church to champion the moral aspect of political issues than it prevents it from educating its members to impregnate such issues with Christian motives. That there are difficulties involved in such an attempt of the Christian group to influence the action of other groups is undeniable, but they are of administration rather than functional.

As an understanding of the individual's relationship with group life develops, and as the individual grows more personal by social contacts, an individual ethic must be supplemented by a group ethic. The Christian must be convinced that the obligations set by his economic, political, and cultural connections as truly call for the embodiment of the spirit of Jesus as individual relations. As the intelligence of its officials and members develops, a church must bring religious faith to bear upon group action. Individual Christians must be made to see that they cannot segregate their morality within certain relations of life, but that it must extend to all. The character of social change will be determined largely by the proportion of the sacrificial spirit of Jesus which is brought into group action. To give justice is more difficult than to demand justice. A church, as a group whose function is to make co-operation with the constructive forces of the universe dependent upon the example and spirit of Jesus, has obligations to make life progressive rather than static, and more personal rather than merely economically efficient. Recognition of the personal worth of the individual rather than the coercive power of the state or any other group, including itself, is involved in its function. If it is ignored a church will be an anachronism to be ignored or destroyed.

III

From the days of Guizot, it has been customary to think of Western civilization as the outcome of the combination of classical civilization, Teutonic independence, and Christianity. For a time, this generalization was threatened by the rise of the economic interpretation of history upon which social theories were built. At present, the historian who has no particular theory to champion can see that western civilization is not the product of any single cause or combination of abstract principles. It has been made by human beings who have found new efficiency by organizing various group activities. The interplay of these groups has been mutually conditioning in that their members were involved in both religious and political activities. The churches have undertaken to fulfill their function of help-gaining relationship with God by means of a developed faith in Jesus as a savior, but they have expressed the social presuppositions and practices of their members.

As the churches merged into vast administrative Catholic units, the clergy, as those believed to have qualifications derived from the apostles which empowered them to represent a church in its sacraments, message, and administration, became increasingly separated from the great mass of Christians, and were recognized as "the Church" itself in its dealing with human affairs. Religious bodies composed of clergy and monks at the same time grew rich. In the course of time a large proportion of the land in western Europe belonged to them. The belief that the Catholic Church could relieve the dead from some of the cleansing sufferings of Purgatory led to the endowment of masses which increased the economic power of religious organizations. Charity became a source of merit. As it was administered under religious auspices, it served to increase the political and social power of a body believed to be the representative of God. In the nature of the case, an institution possessed of wealth could be counted on to maintain the *status quo* and oppose changes which limited its prerogatives and power. The clergy were tried only in clerical courts. They were free from taxes and military duties. They gave legitimacy to marriage, and by their power of excommunication controlled the action, not only of the common people, but of the nobility, and in some cases even of kings.

This combination of economic and supernatural resources made organized Christianity a factor in European affairs.

Any estimate of the medieval Catholic Church should not overlook the contribution which it made through its support of art, its religious houses and the universities, to the maintenance of the classical heritage and the supremacy of spiritual values. In a day when the state controlled social processes by military power, the Roman Church saved Western Europe from the decay which threatened it by its hostility to culture represented by Moslems and Jews. Further, independent Catholic thinkers undertook to organize thought and social interests in less rigorously ecclesiastical lines. Their influence, however, did not produce marked change within those circles in which the clergy had political and economic influence. The extravagance of high ecclesiastics in the fifteenth and sixteenth centuries increased their economic pressure upon the people at large and resulted in the break which may fairly be called the Protestant Revolution. In it, political and economic, as well as ecclesiastical elements are to be seen.

The accumulated wealth of the clergy undoubtedly had an influence in the shaping up of capitalism. Although it was not on the whole unfavorable to commercial development, the Roman church undertook to prevent interest, which was regarded as usury. It was, however, unable to prevent the loan of capital, and finally had to compromise by opposing excessive usury. The Calvinist movement gave new legitimacy to such philosophy and practices, largely because it developed among cities, where commercial and financial interests were much more marked than in regions which were agricultural and feudal. Capitalistic thrift was justified as a means of doing good.

The history of Western civilization shows how the possession of power by those who regard themselves as the agents of moral idealism leads to reliance upon methods incompatible with their professed aims. In the name of God, crusaders fought and massacred Moslems, Albigensians, and Eastern Christians; the Inquisition brought wholesale death to heretics; the Church was involved in the political massacre of Huguenots on St. Bartholomew's Eve. The Eastern Orthodox churches have opposed liberty of thought and social progress; the Protestant State Churches have restrained Nonconformity. One has only to recall the treatment of dissent in England, the persecution of the Arminian clergy after the Synod of Dort, the restrictions placed upon religious minorities in Lutheran countries, to realize that religious liberty and social progress have been opposed by churches. The ancient, medieval, and in America, some modern churches have championed slavery. Ecclesiastical opposition has been made to democracy, the extension of the rights of women, legislation protecting women laborers, birth control, divorce, and the restriction of child labor.

CHURCHES AS MORAL FERMENTS

These unpalatable facts must be faced by those who claim that the future of civilization depends upon "the Church," and those who adopt the slogan of a non-social gospel that "the Church" is over against the world. Human welfare is dependent upon the co-operation of many groups. Changes in economic and political life have been the source of most readjustments in human relations. When a social order ceases to be agricultural, it must become industrial; when it ceases to be feudal, it becomes nationalistic; when it ceases to be democratic, it becomes a dictatorship. Whatever influence organized Christianity has exerted in these changes in Western history has not been that of initiation, but of moral direction given them by individuals and minorities nourished within the Church. These have seen the meaning of the values which an ecclesiastical organization either has not seen or, through lack of sympathy with the proposed changes, has been unwilling to apply. An ecclesiastical organization is always tempted to become an end in itself, rather than to serve as a group having a definitely moral and religious function to perform in co-operation with, and for the benefit of, other groups.

Especially is this true of the relation of churches to those intellectual movements which we merge under the term of science. The fact that all churches have treated the Bible as an authoritative divine revelation has given religious value to scientific conceptions of the time in which the Biblical material was produced. Any description and explanation of facts out of accord with these inherited concepts has been treated as anti-religious. During centuries in which the responsibility for education was believed to be that of churches, little room was found for scientific experiment. Those who attempted it were charged with partnership with Satan or punished as enemies of revelation. There probably is no scientific discovery and hypothesis having major importance that has not been condemned by ecclesiastical authority, both Catholic and Protestant. From Galileo and Copernicus to Darwin, the scientist has been opposed by religious authority. The intellectual awakening of the Renaissance was not within the area of empiricism. Art and literature, rather than experimentation, were its chief interests. It is not surprising that the Catholic clergy should have been urged by Pope Leo XIII to revive the teaching of Thomas Aquinas, or that modernism, with its recognition of scientific discovery and methods, should have been condemned by Papacy and Protestant fundamentalist alike. The simple fact is that when a group erects its formulas into an orthodoxy, any proposal of change is of the nature of *lèse majesté*.

Such inhibitions of the churches are largely due to the persistence of imperialism and unconstitutional sovereignty in their doctrines and programs. But none the less in all religious bodies there have been creative minorities and individuals who, often at the expense of persecution, have endeavored to show that the values which the teaching and life of Jesus embodied could best be experienced when brought into a relationship with an increasing knowledge of reality. Religious authority has continued, but the spiritual values which it would preserve have been extended to conditions which it has opposed. It is no accident that the freedom of Christian idealism should have been most widely exercised where democracy was evolving. Wherever political liberalism has been crushed, Christianity itself has suffered. Only an inept student of social process can fail to see the threat to the worth of the individual person in a state that is ecclesiastically, politically, or economically totalitarian. The refusal of so many of the states of continental Europe to permit the progressive minorities and individuals to share in cultural, economic, and political trends has resulted in the anti-religion of Russia, and the anti-Christianity of Naziism. When one group refuses to co-operate and seeks to control other groups in a social order, it consolidates opposition of these other groups and finds itself the victim of its own ambition. There has never been political freedom where there was no religious freedom.

IV

In most discussions of the relation of Church and State, the underlying presuppositions of democracy are lacking. In consequence a church exists as an independent organization co-ordinate with a state, at times, opposing a state. Sharp enmities are born when political and ecclesiastical practice depend upon a social structure in which sovereignty resides not in the people, but in a class or family. A church as a self-directing organization is not the expression of a popular will, but of a supernaturally established autocracy. With such underlying conceptions, the relations of Church and State will always be different from those of free churches with the government of a republic. Religious liberty has never been initiated by church authority in countries where Catholicism or state Protestantism has existed. The political, economic, and religious rights of minorities have not been recognized. We can admire the struggle of the tax-supported German churches to maintain their right to exist as religious bodies, but we could hold them in still higher respect if they had been equally opposed to the persecution of the Jews. There can be little hope for the effectual application of the principles of love to political affairs under such conditions. The organization of a state, and the basic conception of citizenship will condition the action of a church in fulfilling its function. As long as its organizing principle is Nicean theology, a church will be committed to the political *status quo*. It is not strange that among the errors listed by Pius IX should be the democratic conceptions of the state and religious freedom. If the history of the Christian churches on the continent of Europe is any criterion, they themselves will have to be aroused to the social significance of their faith in a God of love, and a realization that charity and promise of Heaven are no proper compensation for economic, political, and racial injustice.

In states where democracy has found expression in religious freedom, churches can be urged to include within their function that of making nations moral units. Such a task involves the education of Christians in the moral obligations of their citizenship. It is idle to expect national altruism in a nation of selfish citizens. When acquisitiveness becomes dominant in citizens, acquisitiveness, rather than justice, will determine a nation's international policy.

Such an extension of the function of churches carries one far ahead of our present conception of nations. For a few years we dared hope that there would be formed a group of nations in which intelligent arbitration, patient discussion, and readiness to give justice as well as to get justice, might characterize international relations. Locarno and the Kellogg-Briand treaties seemed to confirm the hope that nations might become moral rather than coercive units. The failure of such hope was due largely to the unpreparedness of nations to embody such ideals—which are obviously involved in love—in their relations. Democracy was impracticable in lands where there were no democrats. The inertia of the past made the correction of injustices and mistakes of the Versailles treaty more difficult because of the indifference of the churches to the social significance of their faith. The world slipped back into the seventeenth century, and consecrated its scientific efficiencies to the building up of armaments. Such a reversal of history makes it all the more imperative that churches in countries where they can fulfill their functions freely should realize the crisis which the world faces. It is not enough for them to oppose war, they must also so educate citizens morally that national policies shall not involve the causes of war. To withdraw from such a task into introspective repentance and æsthetic worship, to wait for God to turn a crisis into a catastrophe, is denial of their function as a group. To bring nations into help-gaining relationship with a creative activity of the universe through the recognition of intelligent love is involved in the function of every church. Before a church can refuse to co-operate with a government on the ground that it must obey the will of God, it must be sure that its convictions and attitudes are genuinely in accordance with the spirit of Jesus, and not simply an attempt to maintain existing conditions. The projection of ecclesiastical prejudices into political issues is a danger to religious liberty. Idealists are always tempted to rely upon police power for the enforcement of their ideals. A church has repeatedly to learn that the ideals of Jesus cannot rest on force. Men must be persuaded and not coerced if love is to be embodied in human society. A state has the obligation of maintaining order, but the experience of centuries shows that an attempt to enforce religious conformity is a threat to individual liberty. On the other hand, to organize churches into political units is as dangerous as for the state to become a religious unit.

It follows that before a religious body can safely champion a political or economic program, it must itself illustrate the ideals it preaches. It must itself be convinced that in the light of an intelligent examination of the data at hand a program is a defensible application of the spirit of love to human affairs and that through it co-operation with the personality-creating activities of the universe is assured. There is always danger that the socialization of the spirit of Christ may be directed by impulse rather than wisdom. No social order is composed of those who are whole-heartedly non-acquisitive. Any attempt on the part of a church, either as an institution or through its members, to embody the principles of Jesus in social action must be realistic. Good men have too often assumed that the members of a social order were convinced as to the desirability of ideal conditions. The fate of prohibition is an object lesson in the unwisdom which lies in substituting reliance upon the state for the educational and inspirational methods of the churches. It is the task of love to implement its idealism wisely. The function of a church is to provide motives which lead to such implementing. Other groups have as their function the embodiment of such motives in intelligent agitation and organization. But such a distribution of function cannot excuse a church for indifference to social evils. It cannot recognize war, or economic injustice, or the suppression of constitutional rights, or the subjection of personal values to impersonal ends, or inter-racial enmities, or the exploitation of the unprivileged, as anything but to be opposed. In the same proportion as it is true to its function does it become sensitive to such evils. One of the most obvious signs of recent years is the development of interest on the part of Christians in such matters. The records of almost every religious body in the United States and of the ecumenical conferences in Stockholm and Oxford, afford plenty of evidence that Christian churches are being aroused to make the ideals of Jesus criteria for the action not only of individuals but of other groups in the social order. Generally speaking, such group pronouncements vary from extreme conservatism to something like economic and political radicalism, but they have in common the realization that churches as social groups cannot detach themselves from social process. This should have been evident enough from the history of the Church. But those whose privileges would be lessened by the democratization demanded by the principles of love have too often so manipulated church groups as to make them champions of the *status quo*. In democracies the danger has not been altogether avoided, but the freedom which the churches there enjoy has enabled them to express a growing sense of the fact that the extension of social morality is involved in their function as religious bodies.

It must be admitted that there is danger that in such social interest a church may regard itself as possessing the same duties as Christian individuals and that it may overlook what is its vitally religious contribution to social change. That contribution is not to program the will of God but to inculcate faith that the way of love is a practicable basis upon which to build a society because it is in accordance with the constructive activities of the universe. Our day needs this faith. In the midst of change it needs a criterion which it can trust. Basic religious faith in a God who, however metaphysically considered, is not out of touch with human affairs, is something more than an enthusiasm for a social theory. A realization that mankind must suffer when out of responsive adjustment to cosmic activities is more constructive than a philosophy of discontent. To base a social order upon coercion and terror is not paganism, but rebellion against the cosmic activity that has made men personal. Misery is inevitable.

V

The changes through which Western civilization has passed have not destroyed the ideal of unity involved in the identity of function of all Christian groups. Though the expectation of a kingdom established by God in some catastrophic fashion was sublimated into the conception of Heaven, Augustine expressed the persistent hope of the Christian churches when he made history a drama of struggle between the Kingdom of God and the Kingdom of Satan. Stripped of its eschatological vestments, such a view is a philosophy of history that sees the churches as God's agents in establishing a world order. The effort to establish a Holy Roman Empire, the repeated crusades to bring the known world under the control of Christians, the claims of Popes to be superior to earthly monarchs, were attempts at reaching such unity. Conditioned by social patterns of a civilization shaped by a union of imperial heritage with Teutonic ruthlessness, official Christianity could see only coercion and destruction as a means of enforcing the will of God. Zealous Catholic sovereigns like Ferdinand and Isabella felt justified in driving Jews from Spain. The New World could be divided by the Papacy between the Catholic rulers of Spain and Portugal. Even the identification of religion with governments in the seventeenth century made military conquest in the name of religion the only recognizable way to European unity. But such tragic reliance upon brutality by the officials of Church and State did not prevent the repeated exposition by individual teachers of the hope for a better social order based upon the teaching of Jesus. Both in the Catholic and in the Protestant writers of the sixteenth and seventeenth centuries, there is repeated application of moral ideals to the state and international affairs. In some cases, plans were proposed for international peace which anticipate those of the League of Nations. Dante and Aquinas had set forth "Christian republics," although they do not agree as to the relations of Church and State. After the discovery of America, and the consequent expansion of the concept of the world, Christian ideals were extended by statesmen and philosophers, as well as by theologians. The literature of the sixteenth century abounds in descriptions of the Christian attitude towards government, war, and property as well as to poor relief education, and reforms of penal institutions. Catholic theologians insisted that business as well as politics, should be brought under the control of Christian principles. The Jesuit Suárez could say that each state "viewed in relation to the human race, is in some measure of that universal unity." Grotius brought religion as well as the laws of nature to bear on the international relations. George Fox and the Society of Friends undertook to establish absolute pacifism.

The fact that these ideals were not put into operation does not obscure the fact that they emerged in Christian circles as an interpretation of the bearing of churches upon human affairs. The basic difficulty in applying them was, as always, persistence of social attitudes and practices which do not spring from altruistic motives or intelligent understanding of human relations. It hardly behooves those who live in our day to pass too severe criticism on these earlier

interpreters of the function of a church. As idealists they are still in advance of modern practices.

VI

The relations of ecclesiastical organizations with
social institutions or groups vary according to the
structure of the social order. Where there has been
no real democracy, as in so many countries of continental Europe, the churches have organized political parties without developing socially-minded individuals. In a thoroughgoing democracy, such methods
are feared. Religious prejudice unfortunately exists,
and in the United States there have been sporadic
outbreaks of religious bigotry. But in assuming political character, a church neglects its own function, and confuses its own task with that of individuals. However much a religious body must give
expression to hostility to the policy that belies personal value, its most significant influence arises from
the fact that its members are also members of other
groups. Indeed, one outstanding significance of a
democratic system is that a person's membership in
one group is not conditioned by his membership in another. In social orders where there are class distinc-
tions, such freedom of action is impossible. It is
therefore all the more important that a church
should not only educate Christians to maintain their
individual morality, but also express in their other
relationships their belief that the principle of love

will give more permanent and better results than coercion. Such an attitude will condemn racial hostility, national enmities and economic class conflict. It
will not only lead to care for the outcast and the un-
derprivileged, but to help to organize social life so
that there will be no outcasts and no underprivi-
leged. The official reports of the Oxford Conference
presume an ecumenicity founded upon the function
of the churches to carry forward the spirit of Jesus
through individuals into our present world order. If
the spirit of Jesus is to be made central in all phases
of life, a church must produce such Christians. A
good social order cannot be organized from selfish
people any more than a marble palace can be built
from mud bricks. It is only in a rhetorical sense that
one can speak of "the Church" as if it were a body
independent of its members. The more one studies
history, the more one comes to feel that Christians
are more influential than Christianity. However important a doctrinal uniformity may be, moral discontent and reliance on the constructive power of
love are the two great contributions which the
church can make to the changing order; but such attitudes are not abstract, but those of individual men
and women. The rise of racial hatred, the collapse
of paper democracies, and the emergence of totalitarian states are in no small measure due to the refusal of churches to recognize the freedom and social responsibility of individuals. The new sense of
Christian unity will not be of more than academic in-

terest unless churches undertake to inspire their members not only to prepare for Heaven, but to see to it that God's will is done on earth as it is in Heaven. The obligations of the individual cannot be assumed by churches, but the education of individuals to express the principles of their religion in their social relations is involved in the function of all churches.

7

ARE CHURCHES STILL NEEDED?

Such a question may appear to be purely rhetorical. In the long perspective of the future, however, it is anything but that. Was there ever a period when there was so much free discussion of religion and interest in its significance on the part of anthropologists, psychologists, physicists, and other members of the fraternity of science? Indeed, it almost seems as if no scientist is quite ready to die until he has written a book on the subject. Philosophers are equally concerned, and "philosophy of life," "search for the good life" or "the will to believe" are as much members of the popular vocabulary as the "haves" and the "have-nots." In all this discussion there is persistent criticism, if not belittling, of churches, generally referred to as "the Church." Among those who hold tenaciously to the conception of "order," this attitude is, of course, not to be discovered, but among strictly Protestant, or rather, non-Catholic, Christians, religious interest is decreasingly ecclesiastical. Religion is given a new extension of definition and may include almost any sort of loyalty, from Communism to Humanism.

139

The explanation of this is not hard to find. On the one hand is tacit, if not expressed, rejection of the religious beliefs which the churches have inherited by those who really share in today's intellectual and social reconstruction. On the other hand scientific charity and other forms of social service assuming a professional character have taken over many of the philanthropic activities of churches.

Much of the interest in religion among our intelligentsia is a revolt against the creedal statements of churches as untenable if not unthinkable. It is doubtless because of this fact that there is a noticeable trend towards a philosophy of religion which is highly individualistic and does not attempt to express the Christian ideals in an ecclesiastical form. The terror of the supernatural upon which so many religions have been built has very largely passed with intelligent people, however much it may exist in the realm of the subconscious, or be explained in the new vocabulary of glands and frustrations and complexes given us by the psychologists. And if religion is only some type of wishful thinking born of a child's love of a father or mother, it is difficult to see why it should be treated seriously. When once men cease to be afraid of the Judgment Day, and no longer fear post-mortem suffering, and can die without obtaining an ecclesiastical passport to Paradise, or at least to a reduction of the period of discipline in Purgatory, why should they be concerned about either "the Church" or churches? Cannot a man be religious on his own? And does not the philosopher tell us that "solitariness" is of its very essence?

I should be the last to deny the worth of those intimate experiences which a rational mystic enjoys. In fact, I conceive of religion as a bio-mysticism in which by the projection of the life process of an individual the human and divine reach adjustment. But such a conception argues the need of appreciating the significance of churches rather than a retreat into a Stoic or Confucian solitariness. One can admire Marcus Aurelius and yet realize that the Christian communities which he, or at least his officials, persecuted, had more significance for the European culture than even his *Meditations* and imperial policy. As a social group, a church has for its particular function today that which it has had in the past. That is to say, it can further the help-gaining adjustment of individuals with those cosmic activities upon which we are dependent, with which we are organically united, and which operate in the personal as well as in the chemical and physical realms to which humanity belongs. Doctrines have rationalized and rites have implemented this recognition of cosmic relations.

Nor does the growth of scientific philanthropy mean that churches are no longer to have a religious function. True, a few radicals hold that social and cultural activity is the primary, if not the only, function of a church. They would substitute sociology and psychology for theology, and social activities, moving pictures, basketball games, political discussions, for the conventional activities of a church. Such a view deprives religion of any other than social validity and makes churches social institutions of the order of Social Settlements, Parent-Teacher Associations, and United Charities.

The delegation of certain forms of social service to well-ordered agencies, really serves to specialize the place of churches in the division of labor among social groups. Back of every institutional activity there lies some spiritual force, without which the institutions themselves would decline. Any institution which can produce people of good will is indispensable if society is to grow better. The church is this sort of institution *par excellence*.

But good will itself demands a basis. Why should the strong care for the weak, or the fortunate care for the unfortunate, unless there be some fundamental reason for this violation of the law of the survival of the physically fittest to survive? In humanity there must be something even more fit than strength, else our care for the weak and the diseased, the depressed and the dependent, may be a weakening of the race itself. Regard for human welfare implies that human welfare is worth preserving.

Churches can be counted on to develop and advance this basis for the correct social attitude. They ground their belief in justice and good will in God. Whether or not individuals may be religious, no one can be so blind as not to see that this conception is tremendously dynamic. Furthermore, it preserves enthusiasm. Cynicism always besets those who have devoted themselves to the amelioration of human sin and stupidity. The church, if not the only, is certainly the chief agency for lifting social duty with its self-sacrifice from professional routine into human brotherhood. It is more blessed to give than to receive when one feels the urge of divine love.

I

Before it can be fairly denied that churches have been outmoded, two presuppositions must be avoided. In the first place, while it is true that the past lives on in the institutions and the attitudes of the present, it is not true that antiquity is synonymous with sanctity. If the history of the Christian movement shows anything, it is that there has always been more or less adjustment of inherited beliefs and practices of churches to changing social conditions, and that where such adjustment has not been made, religious inheritance has relied upon authority rather than upon reason. Only as dogma is viewed as a temporal rationalization of a permanent value can it be respected by those who are unwilling to make submission to ecclesiastical authority a source of religious security. That millions of people find security in such implicit faith is obvious, but Christianity can be creative only when its representatives extend its faith in the love dramatized in Jesus into social process.

In the second place, the function of churches as

social groups must be distinguished from the duties of individual Christians. That conclusion is clearly derived from the history of Christian religion. Any confusion at this point is as misleading as would be to confuse the function of a school with the duties of those it educates. Nothing will be gained, and indeed, much will be lost, if "the Church" is used as a synonym for Christians. Liberally minded Christians especially need to be convinced that the churches have a religious function which is not that of other socially-minded groups.

II

Christians need churches to show that love is a practicable basis for social action. By love is not meant liking. If the full significance of Jesus be understood, it is obvious that the Christian can love people he does not like. Such an attitude is more than mutuality, for the Christian, like his Master, must love his enemies. It is more than affection, and it is not acquisitive like the desires of sex. It is a sacrificial social-mindedness which endeavors to share privileges. The efforts which earnest souls have repeatedly made to find spiritual satisfaction in solitariness have broken down either in some psychopathic lapse or in group action. I remember once, as I was traveling down the Wady Kelt, which lies between Jerusalem and Jericho, I asked my guide what the collection of shacks up on the side of the hill might be. "That," he said, "is a colony of hermits."

A church is the outgrowth of this co-ordinating impulse which lies in the Christian experience. However unintelligent their ideas of salvation and their rationalization of conduct may have been, Christians have organized themselves in groups. All religions are forms of social behavior, but the Christian churches are needed as manual training schools of the Christian spirit in the life of groups.

III

Christians need churches for the appropriation of God through social experience. It is not only, in the words of the hymn, that Christians "share their mutual woes"; they also share a God reached through a participation in group solidarity. A religious body in maintaining worship develops corporate emotion in which individuals share. For that reason, the forms and practices which have acquired the power to suggest emotional qualities are not to be judged too critically. As a distinguished English theologian once said, one can chant creeds which one can not say. And the reason doubtless is, that by them one enters into a fellowship with the past, and so carries forward no mystical communion with the saints, but a persistent attitude which makes the soul open to the influence of the divine. The God discoverable in the complicated processes of the universe is discoverable in the group of those who, with such intelligence as they may have, embody the unifying influence of love.

The reliance of Protestantism upon the Bible has led to an overemphasis on the doctrinal aspect of our religion, and a neglect of the church as a medium of divine activity. Yet in the controversial period of Protestantism when men were seeking truth and protesting against error, emotional fervor was born of theological discussion and a sense of group solidarity. That men failed to realize all the bearings of such experience was due very largely to the inhibitions set by practices of the social order in which they lived.

The emotion derived from group attitude makes the individual life particularly susceptible to the personal influence of God. However we may define the term, God stands for our conceptions of the cosmic personality producing activity which man does not originate, but with which he is organically connected. Such activity may not be any more thoroughly understood than that which we call electricity, or matter itself. But mankind has found ways of responsive adjustment. Participation in a religious group is one of these. A Christianity without a Church might have its value as a philosophy, but it would deprive men of those divine influences which come through the group.

IV

Christians need churches as groups which are specifically endeavoring to appreciate and inculcate the

spirit of Jesus Christ by substituting service for acquisitiveness. The appeal of Jesus was always to the
privileged to share their privileges. In a social order
like ours, institutions which struggle for the rights
of their members are indispensable; but the struggle
for rights invariably leads to conflict and, too often,
to coercion and oppression. The spirit of Jesus is not
one of getting justice, but of giving justice. However
crude a doctrine of an atonement may be, and however magical the use of the crucifix and the cross
may appear, they are constant reminders of the sacrificial idealism of Jesus. To educate people as to
the real significance of this spirit, and its bearing
upon all human relations, is a task demanding the
Christian co-operation which a church represents.

v

Churches are needed for the reason that social
groups can preserve values which otherwise might
be dissipated. Members join a movement and share
in these values. Public opinion can be shaped by
newspapers and radio and other means of propaganda, but such propaganda to be effective must find
expression in group action. When once it is institu-
tionalized a belief becomes contagious. Unless there
are institutions that actually conserve values by their
own ongoing, the influence of Christian principles
will be less felt in social process.

There is just now a curious renascence of a feeling that "the Church" must stand over against the world and condemn it. According to some proponents of this anti-social gospel, Christians should neither accept political office nor enter politics. Such proposals are nothing new. History abounds in groups that have endeavored to divorce themselves from the State, on the ground that their subjection to God did not want their participation in government, or even the rituals of patriotism. The spirit of the monastic orders was much the same. They withdrew from the ordinary procedure of life, but they never succeeded in utterly breaking with the State. One has only to think of the significance of a man like Bernard of Clairvaux to realize how futile is the attempt of Christian organizations to separate themselves from the social process.

The relationship of churches to society is supplemental to their task of sending out their individual members to express Christian ideals to other social groups. They can denounce evils which their membership can help to remedy. They can exert a direct influence upon other group life not simply because they stand for ideals that are sound, but because they believe in activities of the universe which will be helpful or destructive according to the relations established with them. A certain type of absolute thinking born of the collectivism and pessimistic distrust of democracy that has swept over Europe, regards such co-operation of church with social process as of the nature of a compromise. But such absolutism is far from a realistic understanding of the world in which we live. Whether they will or not, Christian organizations have influence, and this influence will be greatly increased as they convince individuals and groups that love is a practicable basis upon which to build human society because God is love. One can see the effect of this conviction in many fields, but probably in none is it more effective than in opposition to war. Other social groups are opposed to war, but churches put this opposition upon more than a humanitarian or economic basis. They represent belief in an orderly universe; in an evolutionary process that must find expression in something more than conflict; in freedom as more permanently constructive than coercion; in cosmic activities with which we are organically connected and which we picture as a God who can be trusted to carry forward any type of life which is intelligently at one with Him.

Churches, in a word, are needed to give social life a basic religious faith as a motive for reform and reconstruction.

In the light of these facts, it is apparent that the need of the hour is not pietism or mysticism in the ordinary sense of the word, not a despairing apocalyptism, not a legislating Jesus who lived in a world radically different from ours, but a concretely organized religion which embodies his spirit, extends it to human relations, and justifies reliance upon the personality producing activities of the universe. The Catholic Churches have this conviction as to their significance. Protestantism needs to regard a church as having a religious power. Fortunately it is regaining a sense of the Christian religion as a common faith to which different peoples and social epochs and economic development have more or less intelligently contributed. The effort to find a creedal basis for such unity is anachronistic. What is needed is a revived sense of the identity of function of Christian churches. They can get together by working together and praying together. Christian co-operation will exhibit a common faith that the God of things which are becoming will continue to act as He did when things became. An intelligent understanding of the past will make plain the need of religion to help the world gain a sense of security and a peace which does not rest upon confronting armaments. This religious potency of ongoing Christian groups true Protestants can share with Catholics. Let men join churches rather than theologies and so be influenced by the God they mediate through the spirit of Jesus they socialize.